The Voice of the People

A deliberative poll takes the two technologies, polling and television, that have given us a superficial form of mass democracy, and harnesses them to a new and constructive purpose—giving voice to the people under conditions where the people can think. Working with WETA, the Washington public broadcasting station, I had proposed a deliberative poll for the beginning of the 1992 primary season to act as a reform for the "invisible primary"—the period when candidates acquire their initial credibility and momentum.[37] However, after an announcement in July 1991, we were unable to raise all the necessary money, and the event was canceled. The Gulf War had delayed serious focus on the coming presidential election, and after the Gulf War, potential sponsors predicted that 1992 would prove an uninteresting election. Over and over I was told, in effect, "What interest will there be in this election when the incumbent has a 90 percent approval rating?"

Disappointed with this result, I went to England on a long-planned sabbatical and managed to persuade the television network Channel 4 and the newspaper the *Independent* to be the first to try out the process on a national basis and on national television.

Roger Jowell, the director of Social and Community Planning Research (SCPR, the independent British research organization that conducted the survey), commented to me, on seeing the entire sample gathered for dinner in one room: "I've selected thousands of national random samples, but I've never *seen* one—no one has." The reason is that by the conventions of survey research, one would never wish to see a sample gathered together. After all, the people might talk to each other: they might discuss the issues and as a result become more informed or change their views. In that sense, they would become unrepresentative of ordinary unreflective public opinion. In my view, they would become representative of something else—representative of the public the people would become if everyone had a comparable opportunity to behave more like ideal citizens and discuss the issues face to face with other voters and with political leaders.

The deliberative poll has not developed in a vacuum. It builds on important work in encouraging citizen deliberation. It also builds on the movement toward public journalism discussed earlier. Most efforts to realize public or civic journalism rely on conventional opinion polling to formulate the "people's agenda," however, and Jay Rosen criticizes the press for having accepted those polls as the appropriate measure of public opinion. He cites the pioneering work of survey researcher Daniel Yankelovich, who distinguishes between "public opinion" and "public judgment." The latter represents what people think, on those occasions when they have had a chance to confront a range of conflicting arguments and conflicting values and arrive, after face-to-face deliberation, at a considered judgment. Public journalism can be thought of as focusing on one single task: "to improve the chances that public opinion will evolve into public judgment."[38]

Yankelovich has spent a productive career as a leading public opinion researcher, conducting sample surveys with the firm that bears his name. But he came to see the superficiality of public opinion and founded, with others, the Public Agenda Foundation, which develops briefing materials designed to facilitate citizen deliberation. The work of the Public Agenda Foundation combined with that of the Kettering Foundation to support the work of a nationwide network of citizen deliberators, the National Issues Forums (NIF). About 3,200 citizen forums around the country are held each year under the auspices of NIF. As David Mathews, the president of the Kettering Foundation, explains, the collaborators in NIF "wanted to develop a different type of public forum, one that would deal with issues from the public's perspective. That meant going beyond technical, ideological and legislative positions to find out how each issue affects what is most valuable to people."[39]

Based on focus groups conducted by Public Agenda, issues are "reframed into three or four options that capture these 'values' or the deeper motivations that are at play. The issue books spell out the consequences of each policy option of what citizens consider most valuable." In thousands of citizen forums around the country, the participants grapple with the pros and cons of each option and see whether, after extensive discussion, they can find any bases for common ground. "The objectives of the forums are to help people to become a public, to develop the skills needed for public politics, to speak in a public voice, and to contribute to defining the public's interests."[40]

The NIF forums facilitate citizen deliberation. But they do so primarily among self-selected groups. Thousands of organizations sponsor them, including "colleges, universities, and secondary schools; libraries and leagues; churches, synagogues, and theological centers; literacy programs and leadership programs; and student associations and senior citizens centers."[41] In all these local settings the discussion is among those who volunteer, agree, or put themselves forward. Hence, the "public voice" of these forums is, inevitably, the voice of that part of the public willing to become engaged in politics, or already engaged. These NIF forums are deliberative, but, given this limitation, they are not representative. Nevertheless, they are an enormously rich and fruitful corrective to conventional opinion polls, which have the opposite problem—they are representative but not deliberative.

Most important, the citizen forums sponsored by NIF and Kettering take us a step closer to a more deliberative and engaged society by providing thousands of citizens with the opportunity and the occasion to think through current issues, to confront trade-offs, and to grapple with the hard choices facing our society. In short, these forums help move a subsection of the country in the direction of public judgment rather than public opinion.

Two representatives of the Kettering Foundation, Bob Kingston and John Doble, helped frame the briefing materials in the British deliberative poll and helped train the moderators for the small group discussion. With similar help, the briefing materials and moderator training for the American project will have the benefit of Kettering and the NIF. In that way, the deliberative process pioneered by NIF in citizen forums around the country can be brought to national television with a statistically representative microcosm to create a public voice that speaks for the people—a public voice that is both representative and deliberative.

We gathered the national random sample for the first deliberative poll, April 15–17, 1994, at the Granada Television Studio in Manchester, England. We attracted participants by paying their expenses, offering them a small honorarium, telling them they would be on national television, and advising them that they would be part of an important experiment in democracy. (We also promised them a chance to visit the sets of the popular prime-time soap opera *Coronation Street* and "Baker Street," where the Sherlock Holmes series is made.)

The sample was selected by scpr from forty randomly chosen polling districts in forty randomly chosen constituencies around the country. First, we conducted a baseline survey in people's homes, face to face. We needed to find out what people thought before they were invited to come to the weekend. We interviewed 869 citizens, randomly chosen from the electoral register. This survey had a high response rate—74 percent. It gives an excellent picture of the public's attitudes on the issue in question: "Rising Crime: What Can We Do about It?" The survey is highly representative of the entire country in age, class, geographical location, gender, education, and every other important dimension. But this baseline survey was not the deliberative poll. It was only the beginning of the process.

Voters were invited to the Manchester event only after they completed the baseline survey. The three hundred who took up the invitation to come to Manchester for the weekend were, in every important respect, indistinguishable from the 869 who took the baseline survey. In terms of class, education, race, gender, and geography the weekend microcosm was fully as representative of the country as the baseline survey. Even more important was the fact that in their attitudes about crime, and in their political positions generally, the weekend microcosm was just as representative of the country as the baseline survey.

One of the persistent claims of critics was that participants who would take up the invitation for the weekend would be precisely the people who were most interested in the issue, specifically, the people who were most fearful of crime. Instead, the weekend sample turned out to be an almost perfect microcosm. Because this sample matched the baseline sample, it was strikingly representative. About 28 percent of both surveys said crime was "not a worry," exactly 21 percent of both surveys considered it "a big worry," roughly 34 percent of the two thought crime "a bit of a worry," and about 18 percent of both surveys said the issue arose only as "an occasional doubt." The weekend sample was no more and no less fearful of crime than the general public, as measured by our baseline survey.

Another speculation was that primarily men rather than women would accept our invitation. We began to worry about this in focus groups we conducted as we were designing the event. In one focus group, a woman said that she "could never consider coming to an event like this." She explained that she had never spent a weekend away from her husband. But in the very next focus group, another woman said she would "definitely come"—because she'd never spent a weekend away from her husband! In the end, of the 300 participants, 150 were men and 150 were women.

As a starting point on the issue of crime, the weekend sample was an almost perfect representation of the nation gathered together in a single place. The challenge for the experiment was whether the participants would change over the course of the weekend. If a deliberative poll gave results identical to an ordinary poll, it would not be worth investing in such an elaborate project again.

Change, however, was not a worry. The members of the sample began to change from the moment they received our invitation. Knowing that they would be on national television, they began discussing the topic with family and friends, they began to read newspapers and listen to the media with more care, they began reading the briefing materials we sent them. Their views thus immediately became unrepresentative of public opinion in the conventional sense. But those views also became representative in an important new sense. They became representative of the views the entire country would come to if it were populated by persons closer to ideal citizens—people who were motivated to be engaged by the issues and who debated them over an extended period. In short their new, considered judgments offered a representation of what the public would think, if it actually had a better opportunity to think about the issue.

During the deliberative weekend, a woman came up to me and said that during thirty years of marriage, her husband had never read a newspaper but that from the moment he had been invited to this weekend, he had changed. Not only did he read every bit of our briefing materials, but he now read "every newspaper every day." She speculated he would be much more interesting to live with in retirement.

The voters who came to Manchester changed in dramatic and coherent ways. They remained tough on crime (they continued to insist that prison should be "tougher and more unpleasant" and that "the death penalty is the most appropriate sentence" for some crimes), but they offered, by the end, a much more complex appreciation of the problem. Realizing the limits of prison as a tool for dealing with crime, they focused on rehabilitation and on different treatments for first-time juvenile offenders. They also increased their sensitivity to the procedural rights of defendants. The "right to silence"—the right to say nothing when questioned by the police and not have that silence held against one in court—for example, showed a dramatic increase in support. Also, opposition to the police's "cutting corners" to secure a conviction increased significantly. In short, the participants demonstrated a new appreciation for the complexity of the issues, the conflicts of values the issues posed, and the limitations of any one solution. Our participants became far more sophisticated consumers of the competing policy prescriptions. They became, at least on this one issue, more thoughtful and engaged citizens.[42] (See the appendix for a summary of some of the results of the deliberative poll.)

What did the event accomplish? It demonstrated the viability of a different form of opinion polling and, in a sense, a different form of democracy. As we have seen, Americans have long struggled with how to adapt democracy to the large nation-state. Face-to-face democracy cannot be applied to large states. Even in Rhode Island, the anti-Federalists could not gather everyone together to hear all the arguments on either side. It was for this reason that the Federalists boycotted the referendum on the U.S. Constitution and said that the only appropriate method for making a decision was the elected state convention. A *representation* of the people, in the form of those elected to go to the convention, would be able to hear all the competing arguments and make an informed decision.

But recall the persistent anti-Federalist worry that no *elected* representation would be representative. Ordinary people like them—farmers, laborers, people without a great deal of education—would tend to get left out. The lawyers and judges and wealthy elite of the day would make the decisions. The elected microcosm, in other words, would not be a genuine microcosm—and might not consider or understand *their* interests.

Democracy, even in the elitist sense of the Founders, was only revived by the notion of elected representation. But another form of representation lay hidden in the dust of history. It was employed by the legislative commissions, citizens' juries and the Council in ancient Athens (the crucial body that set the agenda for meetings of the citizen Assembly). This other method was selection by lot or random sampling. In one sense the use of random sampling in politics was revived by opinion polling. After all, what is a random sample, at bottom, but a lottery? But in the ancient Greek form, and in the form employed in the deliberative poll, opinions are taken not from isolated citizens but from citizens meeting together, deliberating on common problems. These polls represent the considered judgments of the polity, not the top-of-the-head reactions of isolated citizens. Institutions that speak for the people need to be both representative and deliberative. The ancient Greek innovation was a random sample of citizens who deliberated together and in that way realized both values. And this is the form I propose to adapt to the television age.

If this new—and very old—form of democracy were employed in

a general election, at the beginning of the primary season, or before a referendum, then the recommending force of the public's considered judgments, broadcast on national television, might well make a difference to the outcome. Recall Samuel Popkin's argument that voters are inclined to follow cues as arbitrary as President Ford's choking on a tamale in San Antonio.[43] Surely, the cues formed from an elaborate deliberative process should be worth paying attention to. When broadcast on national television and disseminated in the press, the deliberative poll can affect the public's conclusions, but it can also affect the way that public frames and understands issues. If televised deliberative polls succeed in communicating the deliberative process, they can help transform the public agenda to the agenda of an engaged public — to an agenda citizens will care about, and be attracted by, because it will be framed in terms that speak to their concerns in ordinary life.

Channel 4 has already announced a Deliberative Poll for the next British General Election. The American project, at the beginning of the presidential selection season, can be expected to have a major effect on candidates and issues. During the invisible primary the national broadcasting of the considered judgments of the entire country, in microcosm, could provide for a more thoughtful and representative way of launching the primary season and launching the debate. In 1992 only 12 percent of Democrats and 8 percent of Republicans in the relevant states participated in the primary process. As we have seen, the arbitrariness in the ordering of the primaries increases the influence of tiny, self-selected electorates in determining the outcome for the rest of us. Furthermore, given the increasing domination of television as the key medium of public discourse, the primary process has become a duel of attack ads and sound bites fighting for the attention of an inattentive public. The deliberative poll would insert a rational dialogue at the start, one that represents the entire country in one room, under conditions where it can think through the issues. Given the increasingly front-loaded character of the primary calendar, approximately 70 percent of the delegates will be selected in seven weeks in 1996: the entire country has been turned into one giant tele-vision battleground, one huge California primary, if you will. The new and constructive use of television offered by the deliberative poll will give us a thoughtful prelude to the accelerated process to follow. The deliberative poll may, in fact, be the one time when the country will be able to pause, take a deep breath, and think through the issues. The rest of the primary season will then proceed with the speed of a shrinking sound bite.

Most ambitiously, the Deliberative Poll can be thought of as an actual sample for a hypothetical society—the deliberative and en-gaged society we do not have. Ideally, we should get everyone think-ing and discussing the issues. But as we have seen the forces of rational ignorance are powerful. Yet although we cannot get every-one actively engaged under most conditions, through the deliberative poll we can do the experiment and get the microcosm engaged—and then broadcast the results to everyone else. Citizens in the microcosm are not subject to rational ignorance. Instead of one insignificant vote in millions each of them has an important role to play in a nationally televised event. With true engagement and attention from the micro-cosm this representation of the public's judgment becomes a voice worth listening to.

One of the key decisions we made in planning the British Delibera-tive Poll sheds light on the experiment's aspirations, both in Britain and in the United States. The problem was the seemingly simple issue of where in the schedule to place the small-group discussions. We struggled with two different models of how these discussions serve the deliberative process. One is by *absorption,* the other is by *activa-tion.* In one model the respondents *absorb* information from compet-ing experts, mull that information over in small groups, and form their conclusions. On this model the participants would spend a great deal of time listening to competing presentations of relevant factual materials and then they would process those materials in small group discussions.

In the second model, we attempt to do something far more ambitious. There, the small group discussions come first, before participants have any contact with experts or politicians. On this strategy, we facilitate the citizens' melding into groups first, identifying their key concerns first, establishing rapport among themselves first, setting the agenda of the questions and concerns they wish to raise first—and only then put them together with the competing experts and competing politicians. The second model, instead of absorbing its agenda from the experts, energizes a public voice coming *from* the citizens so that it can speak *to* the elites. This strategy was followed in the Manchester experiment, and it set an example for how we hope to conduct future deliberative polls.

At the National Issues Convention, scheduled for mid-January 1996, we intend to identify, far in advance, several key issue areas, based on analyses of such standard public opinion research as polls and focus groups. We shall use standard public opinion research because we are interested in beginning where the public begins. We must select issues that speak to the people's concerns and that facilitate posing the problems in terms they can understand. Working with the Kettering Foundation and the Public Agenda Foundation, we shall adapt briefing materials appropriate for ordinary citizens as an initial background on the issues. Those briefings will be reviewed for both balance and accuracy by a distinguished bipartisan committee chaired by former Democratic Congresswoman Barbara Jordan and former Republican Congressman Bill Frenzel. Candidates who wish to provide materials on these issues will be invited to do so. We expect that the citizens invited to participate will prepare seriously for the event. Knowing that they will be on national television, and knowing that the issues are important, they are likely to read the materials, discuss the issues with friends and family, and pay more attention to the media. From the moment they are invited, they begin to become unrepresentative of mass opinion as it is. But they begin to become representative of our ideal public.

The logic is very simple. If we take a microcosm of the entire country and subject it to a certain experience, and if the microcosm (behaving in the way we would like ideal citizens to behave in seriously deliberating about the issues) then comes to different conclusions about those issues, our inference is simply that if, somehow, the entire country were subjected to the same experience as the microcosm, then hypothetically the entire country would also come to similar conclusions.

Of course, it is unlikely the entire country ever would approximate the experiences of a deliberative poll. Even when there is an intense debate, it may well be dominated by attack ads and misleading sound bites. But the point is that if, somehow, the public were enabled to behave more like ideal citizens, then the deliberative poll offers a representation of what the conclusions might look like. That representation should have a prescriptive value. It is an opportunity for the country, in microcosm, to make recommendations to itself through television under conditions where it can arrive at considered judgments.

Earlier I emphasized four democratic values—deliberation, nontyranny, political equality, and participation. I noted that efforts to fully realize all four have usually been unsuccessful. In particular, the move toward mass democracy—a move realized by increasing participation and political equality—has had a cost in deliberation. By transferring the effective locus of many decisions to the mass public, the system is far less deliberative than it would have been had those decisions been left in the hands of elites—elected representatives and party leaders. The deliberative poll, however, offers a *representation* of a democracy that meets all four conditions. With a deliberative atmosphere of mutual respect, tyranny of the majority is unlikely. When all the citizens are effectively motivated to think through the issues, when each citizen's views count equally, and when every member of the microcosm participates, the other three values are realized as well. Fully realizing those values throughout the entire society may be hypothetical. But we can see, in microcosm, what deliberation, political equality, participation and non-tyranny would look like.

Suppose, hypothetically, that the new institution of Deliberative Polling somehow became as accepted a part of our public life as, say, conventional polling is today. Deliberative Polling at the state and local level need not be unusual or expensive. Transportation is a key component of the expense on the national level, and local deliberative polls would not face such a hurdle.

The experience of serious citizen deliberation seems to have a galvanizing effect on the participant's interest in public affairs. So far the evidence for this proposition has been largely anecdotal, but we hope to study this phenomenon systematically in follow-ups with participants in the British project. Suppose, for the sake of argument, that there is a *continuing* effect. In the same way that the citizen mentioned earlier was galvanized to read "every newspaper every day," we might imagine that he continues to be a far more engaged citizen—discussing public issues with others, being more aware of the media, and becoming more likely to participate in public or civic affairs. If Deliberative Polls ever became a staple of public life, we would end up with a society of more seriously engaged citizens—one which was not just a *representation* of how all four democratic values could be achieved but rather an *embodiment* of their achievement. Just as the apparatus of selection by lot in ancient Athens involved so many citizens, so often, that it seems to have galvanized an active citizenry, it is not inconceivable that selection by lot for Deliberative Polls could, someday, have the same effect on our country.

It is not inconceivable, but it is, admittedly, unlikely. Such a flourishing of a new institution is clearly utopian, even as a matter of aspiration. But the image helps clarify an ideal—a picture of the reconstructed role of citizen, not just on television but in actual life. At a minimum, the deliberative poll can articulate the considered judgments of an informed citizenry and broadcast those conclusions to the nation. It provides a different, and more thoughtful, public voice. Other innovations and other institutions would have to be relied on if we are to create a seriously engaged mass citizenry as a routine part of our national life.

When George Gallup articulated his vision for the original opinion poll, it was to "restore" the democracy of the New England town meeting to the large nation-state. He thought the poll would put everyone in one enormous, metaphorical room, where they could think through the issues. Radio and newspapers would communicate the views of elites and the views of citizens would be communicated back by the opinion poll. But the room, the "one great room" of the entire country connected by the media, was too large—so large that no one was listening. People tuned out because the large room fostered rational ignorance. And, apart from national crises, they often tune out, as we can see from nearly half a century of public opinion research since.

The Deliberative Poll, however, attempts to fulfill Gallup's initial aspiration to somehow adapt the New England town meeting, the image of serious face-to-face democracy, to the large nation-state. In doing so it purports to overcome rational ignorance and represent us all. But even if this new departure succeeds, it is not a panacea. Remember that in our discussion of *Magic Town* there were two distinctive outcomes—first, the people felt a responsibility to form considered judgments because they spoke for the nation; second, they helped create an engaged community, where they could work together in a spirit of mutual sacrifice for public causes. In effect, they created social capital.

Without functioning communities of engaged citizens, television programs, by themselves, have limited impact. They may suffer the fate of the initial series published by the *Ledger-Enquirer,* which fell on deaf ears because the community was not prepared for such a dialogue. Television can be a catalyst, but it cannot, by itself, change the country. It can only begin to change the discussion.

175

To make a democracy that works, we need citizens who are engaged, communities that function, and media that speak *for* us as well as *about* us. If we pay attention to the conditions under which citizens become reconnected to political life, we can create a public worthy of public opinion—and public judgment. It would indeed be "magic town" if we brought such a spirit to the entire country.

AFTERWORD

The National Issues Convention
and Beyond

In January 1996, Deliberative Polling[1] became a reality in the United States. For the first time, a national random sample of Americans was gathered in a single place, the University of Texas at Austin, to deliberate on issues facing the country on the eve of the presidential election season.[2] This event, the National Issues Convention (NIC), was many things at once—a social science experiment, a new form of public consultation, a contribution to the media dialogue, and a prelude to the presidential campaign.

We faced a number of challenges for which there were few precedents. First, could we get a representative, random sample of the entire country to participate? Second, what would happen on the weekend? In particular, would the views of the participants be significantly different after the experiment? Would Deliberative Polling produce results different from those of ordinary polls? Third, would the event offer a distinctive contribution to the public dialogue? The gathering of a national random sample of people to a single place would provide an occasion for media coverage of citizen voices in a new way. How much of this potential would be realized? Fourth, what would it mean? Critics had speculated that the Deliberative Poll was a unique media event and that its results would be impossible to replicate. Fifth, there remained a practical question: would Deliberative Polling lead to a continuing research program, or would it prove an expensive, one-shot experiment?[3] What other applications for the process might emerge? I will attempt to sketch answers to these questions here.[4]

1. WOULD THEY COME?

We faced a formidable challenge in attempting to get a representative, national random sample to meet in a single place. Ordinary surveys simply contact respondents by phone or in person. In the case of the NIC, we were asking respondents, after completing an initial questionnaire, to come away for an entire weekend on a specific date, January 19–21, 1996. We had no flexibility about the date or the respondents. Once a respondent was selected, no one could be substituted for that respondent.

We had, of course, our experience from the 1994 and 1995 British Deliberative Polls on which to draw. But Britain is a relatively compact geographical entity—we could conveniently transport the entire sample by bus or by train to the Granada television studio in Manchester. The American project presented a challenge of continental scale. The National Opinion Research Center's (NORC, at the University of Chicago) national random sample would probably include either Alaska or Hawaii, and, in any case, respondents would have to come thousands of miles to a part of the country—Texas—that many would view as unfamiliar.

From our British experience, we knew that we needed to offer a number of incentives. After the initial survey, we told respondents that they were invited to an important national event; that their transportation, meals, and hotel accommodations would be paid for; and that they would receive $300 as a token of appreciation. Most important, we let them know that their voices would matter in a major event on national television. Jim Lehrer of PBS's *NewsHour,* who would serve as host for

the event, recorded a videotape that described the event and asked respondents to take the invitation seriously. This video was played for respondents after the invitation was extended following completion of
the initial questionnaire.

NORC used the same sampling frame as the one employed for its
highly regarded General Social Survey (GSS). Households were chosen
randomly from one hundred sampling points around the country, and
the actual respondent in each household was selected by using a Kish
procedure, a random method, to determine which adult member of the
household would be asked to complete the initial survey. The original
sample had 1,534 addresses, but this included 256 addresses that were
ineligible (the address was not a household, or was vacant, or the people living at the address did not speak English).[5] From the remaining
1,278 households, NORC conducted initial interviews in the fall of 1995
with 914 respondents, a response rate of 72 percent.[6] While this was
slightly lower than the response rate NORC had usually obtained on the
GSS or other surveys, this was a high response rate compared with that
of most surveys. Commercial survey houses do not standardly count
the people they fail to reach in the denominator when they count response rates, but NORC's 72 percent counts the percentage of all the addresses validly in the sample. Because 460 people actually came to the
weekend, the overall participation rate was about 36 percent—as low
as many commercial surveys when their response rates are properly
calculated, but lower than we had hoped. The important issue, however,
is whether the weekend sample turned out to be representative, and
here the research design—which permitted us to compare the weekend
respondents with the entire baseline survey of 914, both attitudinally
and demographically—provided us with plenty of data to allay our
concerns.

Before we launched the initial interview phase, *Parade* magazine
and American Airlines sponsored a contest to give away a small number of trips for citizens to observe the National Issues Convention. This
contest, which was entirely separate from the recruitment of delegates

(all of whom came from NORC's national random sample), provided the occasion for an article in *Parade* about the upcoming event. This article and others in newspapers around the country helped the interviewers to establish the credibility of the event for respondents.

Nevertheless, the offer of a free trip easily engenders suspicion, and some respondents remained skeptical. One respondent, in upstate New York, called his congressman's office to find out if the invitation was on the level. The congressman's office was not familiar with the NIC but suggested that he call the New York State Attorney General's Office to find out if they knew about the event. From there, our respondent was referred to his local PBS station. The PBS station manager congratulated him, saying that the station was indeed broadcasting a program called the *National Issues Convention,* and that he should be very pleased to have been chosen. The respondent switched from skepticism to anticipation in an instant, asking whether he should call a news conference because he definitely would be attending!

Once we overcame the credibility hurdle there remained many practical difficulties. A woman on a farm in Alabama initially refused to attend because there was no one available to milk her cow. She agreed to come only when NORC arranged for her cow to be milked in her absence. One woman said that she initially decided to come because she thought there would be hot water in the hotel! The weekend had other poor people, but in a proportion representative of the country. A quarter of the total participants had family incomes under $20,000 (which matched our baseline poll and census data). Another respondent had never been out of Chicago and had never flown on an airplane (like more than one hundred of the participants). To reassure her NORC arranged for one of her close friends to accompany her. When the pair expressed uncertainty about how to get to the airport, we arranged for a car to pick them up.[7] A couple of weeks after the NIC, she called me to say that the experience was so valuable that her discussion group was talking about organizing a reunion—to travel at their own expense as observers to the next National Issues Convention.

New York Times reporter Steve Holmes followed the saga of recruitment. With NORC's permission he accompanied an interviewer as she approached a potential delegate from Delaware. As the car, with reporter and photographer, pulled up to the selected address in a trailer park in Delaware, children in the neighborhood began to shout, "She won the Publishers' Clearinghouse!" They were right that the respondent had won a kind of lottery, but not one with the prize that they imagined. A woman, sole occupant of the dwelling, answered the door but immediately closed it again, saying that she did not "talk with people." After several conversations in the doorway, in which the respondent characterized herself as a recluse, "Veda" eventually agreed to the interview. Veda's reluctance to be interviewed and her eventual decision to attend the National Issues Convention were described in Holmes's story.[8] At the NIC, a woman came up as I exited one of the sessions and embraced me warmly. "I'm Veda," she said. "Veda from Delaware?" I asked, surprised, but remembering Holmes's article. As we talked it became clear that this woman, who normally talked to very few people, had found her dialogue with so many diverse people an exhilarating experience. "I will never read the words 'we the people' in the same way again," she later told a NORC researcher on the phone.

The difference between a national random sample and the kinds of people who volunteer for televised "town meetings" was dramatized for me by the fact that Veda characterized herself as a recluse. Such a person would never have turned up in a self-selected television audience or in a quota sample. While she voted regularly, she said that her strong opinions tended to "get her into trouble."

Veda, the woman on the farm in Alabama, and the woman from Chicago who had never traveled on an airplane were all part of America in microcosm gathered in a single place. The representativeness of the weekend participants could be evaluated, both attitudinally and demographically, by comparisons to the entire baseline survey and by comparisons to census data. Our weekend microcosm had slightly more westerners, fewer respondents over age seventy, and fewer respondents who had only a high school education—as compared with both the baseline poll or with the country as a whole. Bad weather on the weekend of the convention and the days immediately preceding it led to cancellations and anxiety about travel, particularly among elderly respondents. The bad weather included snowstorms in Minnesota, Wisconsin, Michigan, North Dakota, and Virginia; ice storms in Kansas; and tornadoes in Louisiana and Arkansas. One respondent was an airport snow removal worker in Wisconsin. On the first day of the convention he phoned to say that because of the storm he had been called in to do emergency snow removal. Later he called to say that after working to clear the airport, he was on his way. Many of the respondents had anticipated the convention for weeks and were determined to come to the event.

The respondents were coming to the convention not because they were politically aware "C-Span junkies" or because they felt especially connected to the political process. There was no statistically significant difference between participants and nonparticipants in their propensity to watch television news. Also, there were no statistically significant differences between participants and nonparticipants on such questions as whether respondents thought they had "a say" in government or whether "politicians are out of touch." While respondents did tend to be slightly more participatory (see Appendix B), the weekend was not composed of the political class or of those who were politically plugged in to the media.

In general, the participants formed an excellent microcosm of the country on most demographic and attitudinal items. For example, on race, gender, religion, income, political affiliation, and their recollections of their 1992 presidential votes, they matched up almost perfectly with the baseline poll and, where relevant, with census data. A more specific test is how the weekend participants compared with the nonparticipants on the policy items that would serve as the subject of the weekend's discussions. On fifty-two of the sixty-six policy items[9] in the survey (79 percent), there were no statistically significant differences between participants and nonparticipants at the .05 level.[10] And on the few policy items for which there were statistically significant differences, such differences were typically small.[11]

The sixty-six policy items covered the three areas for discussion at the NIC. For example, on the *family issues* there were no significant differences on such items as government help with childcare, support for parental leave, government assistance to poor families, and moral education in the schools. In *foreign policy* there were no significant differences on use of U.S. troops elsewhere, improving the global environment, and preventing the spread of weapons. In *economic policy* there were no significant differences on such issues as what the tax rates should be, and on budget spending on foreign aid or law enforcement. Even for an item that would be of special concern to the elderly, such as support for Social Security, there were no statistically significant differences between the weekend sample and the nonparticipants.

Hence, even though there were some small demographic differences between the weekend sample and the entire baseline poll, the weekend sample offered a good representation of the country's views on the policy issues to be discussed. While the sample was not perfect, it was certainly the best scientific random sample of U.S. citizens ever gathered in a single place.

2. WHAT HAPPENED?

Getting the sample there was only the beginning. For months we carefully prepared for the group discussions. The National Issues Forums (NIF), with support from the Kettering Foundation, consults more than three thousand citizen groups on the topics that will be employed each year in forums it coordinates around the country. These forums are conducted by a variety of civic organizations, libraries, churches, community colleges, and even prisons. Public Agenda, a New York–based research organization, carefully develops discussion materials for those forums after conducting extensive focus groups and group discussions.[12] This process was far advanced in the summer of 1995, when we had to reach decisions about the issue areas for the convention. We decided that it would make sense to coordinate the topics of the convention with the topics slated for discussion by citizen forums. NIF participants around the country would have the opportunity to watch the convention's proceedings on television and hear presidential candidates respond to questions from a representative sample of citizens briefed with materials that were similar to those being employed in the local discussions. Believing that the National Issues Forums make a real contribution to the democratic dialogue, we also hoped that the televised event would spark further interest among citizens because of the opportunity provided by such forums. The television event (NIC) and the local discussions (NIF) were connected by similar materials, similar discussion methods, similar moderators, and identical topics. To the extent that a serious public dialogue occurs not just on television but also in communities around the country, deliberative democracy has a chance of taking hold.

These practical advantages of coordination only enhanced our delight on learning that the three issues chosen by NIF for the election year were the economy, America's role in the world, and the current state of the American family. We felt that these issues would provide a good basis for discussion with the candidates and a good mixture of issues for the experiment and for the televised dialogue. A review committee of distinguished representatives of both parties was consulted to approve the adaptation of the NIF materials for our convention. This committee, co-chaired by former Democratic Representative Barbara Jordan[13] and by former Republican Representative Bill Frenzel, reviewed the materials for balance and accuracy. It also approved our efforts to shorten the briefings so that our respondents would not be overwhelmed with material on three issue areas in a single weekend (see Appendix G).

The National Issues Forums also contributed the moderators for the thirty small groups into which the convention would divide for deliberations on the weekend. The Kettering Foundation sponsored an orientation in Dayton, Ohio, for moderators, who were selected from National Issues Forums around the country. The moderators had to adapt to some of the special circumstances of the NIC. For example, part of the plan for the weekend, as in the other Deliberative Polls, was for the participants to formulate key questions that they wanted to ask of competing experts and politicians. Getting a consensus on the questions, and on who should ask them, was a task that had to be integrated into the moderator training. Unlike other forums, however, the task required a consensus on the questions but not on the answers. At the end of the weekend the respondents' views on the issues would be assessed in confidential questionnaires. We wanted to insulate the participants as much as possible from the social pressures of reaching a consensus on the substance.

With these preparations the delegates to the NIC gathered in Austin on Thursday evening. They were welcomed to the convention by Jim Lehrer (anchor for the broadcast), Robert Berdahl (president of the University of Texas at Austin), and Governor George W. Bush of Texas. They were shown video summaries of the issues that were keyed to the briefing documents, and then they met in their randomly assigned small groups. The small group discussions focused at length on each issue area, with the ultimate product of each session being questions for the competing experts and the competing politicians. Some of the questions were unexpected: "To whom do we owe the national debt?" Some reflected the small group discussions' efforts to grapple with tradeoffs. When asking about the gap between rich and poor, the question was not just "Can we narrow that gap?" but "Can we narrow that gap and still keep a free-market economy?" When asking about a tax break for the middle class the question was not just how large it would be, but, "How would you structure the tax code and government spending so we can balance the budget and give middle-class Americans a break?"

The format was designed for extensive follow-ups. The idea was that citizens, armed with the authority of the group discussions, would feel more confident in pursuing the question beyond the initial exchange of sound bites. For the event there were three panels of experts and four Republican presidential candidates on the Saturday broadcast[14] (Senator Richard Lugar, publisher Steve Forbes, Senator Phil Gramm, and former Governor Lamar Alexander).[15] The Sunday morning broadcast was a one-hour dialogue with Vice President Al Gore. He was so clearly engaged in listening to the participants, rather than lecturing to them, that he asked for a show of hands on issues like support for the minimum wage. Lehrer had to admonish the vice president that he was getting into the "Deliberative Polling business"—a dimension of the experiment that was better reserved for the official survey of the convention.

At the end of the weekend the participants filled out the same questionnaire that they had filled out when they were first contacted—plus a few questions on their views of the experiment. There were dramatic changes from their initial responses. Out of sixty-six policy items, thirty-one (47 percent) changed significantly at the .05 level.[16] These sixty-six items do *not* include six other items that measured the sense of civic engagement—items such as whether the respondent believes that public officials "care a lot about what people like me think," or that "people like me don't have any say about what the government does." Responses to these items also changed dramatically.[17]

Of course, there was even more change in the sense that on some questions, respondents moving one way canceled out respondents moving the other way, so that there was "churn." Of the sixty-six policy questions, at least 40 percent of the respondents offered a different answer on forty out of the sixty-six policy items (61 percent) and at least 30 percent of respondents offered a different answer on sixty-two out of sixty-six of the items (94 percent). We are including among these changes the movement from "don't know" to having an opinion because one of the crucial dynamics in the Deliberative Poll is the opportunity to form an opinion on a matter that one had not previously considered.[18]

As in other Deliberative Polls, the changes did not conform to ideological stereotypes. For example, while there was a move toward increasing expenditures for childcare and education, as liberals would advocate, there was also a dramatic move toward turning the "safety net for welfare and health care" to the states to "let them decide how much help to give"—a key conservative tenet. Over the weekend respondents were discussing the substantive issues without tying them to "liberal" or "conservative" labels, and the conclusions they came to, on reflection, would provide comfort to supporters from both camps.

The respondents also achieved a clear sense of greater civic engagement over the course of the weekend. There was a twenty-eight-point increase in those strongly agreeing that "I have opinions about politics that are worth listening to" (from 40 percent to 68 percent) and a nineteen-point increase in those agreeing that "public officials care a lot about what people like me think" (from 41 percent to 60 percent).

How did they evaluate the proceedings? When asked to rate the experience on a one to nine scale, from one ("generally a waste of time" to nine ("an extremely valuable experience"), 73 percent gave it a perfect nine. When asked to evaluate components of the weekend as "very valuable," "somewhat valuable," or "little or no value," 82 percent thought that the group discussions were very valuable, 65 percent thought that talking with other delegates outside the group discussions was "very valuable," and 42 percent thought that "the sessions with the political leaders on TV" were "very valuable." As for the conduct of the group discussions, 79 percent agreed strongly that "the group leader provided the opportunity for everyone to participate in the group discussion," and 79 percent disagreed strongly that "the group leader often tried to influence the group with her or his own views" (see Appendix F).

We will return to the substantive results in Section 5. In the meantime, let us note two other components of the experiment: a control group and a follow-up with respondents several months later. With support from the Pew Charitable Trusts, NORC was able to conduct a separate telephone poll of an RDD (random digit dial) sample with many of the same questions from our questionnaire at the time of the broadcast. The point was to see whether the changes we observed at the convention resulted from the experiment or were occurring anyway in public opinion. The results, which will be the subject of a separate report, generally support the view that the changes we observed at the convention were in fact the results of the process. They were not changes that were occurring anyway in public opinion at the time. This separate sample makes the experimental design of the NIC conform to the "post-test only control group" recommended in the classic work of Campbell and Stanley.[19] We also hope to incorporate this feature in other Deliberative Polls planned under conditions of high media visibility.[20]

The Pew Charitable Trusts also supported a follow-up by NORC at the time of the November election with members of the sample. In addition, this evaluation supported reinterviews with a randomly selected portion of the nonparticipants. Separate data analysis of these two follow-ups is under way. Currently, we can get some insight into whether the changes in Deliberative Polls persist from the data in Appendix E, which resulted from a reinterview ten months later of respondents in the first Deliberative Poll on crime in Britain. There was a pattern. Let us call Round 1 the initial survey at time of recruitment, Round 2 the survey at the end of the weekend, and Round 3 the follow-up ten months later. There is a pattern of considerable persistence in Round 2 opinions, but also some return to earlier views. In each case Round 3 falls more or less midway between Round 2 and Round 1.[21] The subjects reached a considered judgment under special stimuli at the end of the convention. They then returned home, with all of its normal environmental influences. Ten months later, their views reflect the combination of these two factors.

3. DELIBERATIVE POLLING AND
THE PUBLIC DIALOGUE

The Deliberative Poll is more than a social science experiment; it is also meant to contribute to the public dialogue. The NIC was designed to resonate with citizen forums, conducted by NIF, all around the United States. It was also meant to make use of the media in a constructive way—one that would connect to the concerns of ordinary citizens once they had a chance to focus on the issues.

The NIC broadcast plans, with scheduled repeats, amounted to nine and a half hours.[22] According to PBS estimates, these broadcasts reached a total of about ten million viewers. Furthermore, the live sessions with the candidates were also simulcast on NPR. The convention was also covered by ABC, CNN, and other broadcast media. In addition, about 350 journalists attended the convention and were permitted to watch the small group discussions as well as the larger plenary sessions. The challenge of covering the convention was great enough that two separate groups organized symposia in Austin for journalists from around the country just to discuss how to cover the event.[23]

As we saw in Chapter 5, a central aspiration of civic or public journalism is to air the people's agenda on the issues. But a limitation of such efforts, thus far, has been the reliance on conventional polling for any determination of what the people's agenda might be. When the people are not paying attention, they may not have any agenda at all. On some issues, polls express only "top of the head" attitudes or even nonattitudes. Deliberative Polling provides an input to civic journalism in that it provides a way of consulting the public once the microcosm has had an opportunity to engage an issue and formulate its concerns. Public journalism requires a public—an engaged community of citizens who can articulate their concerns. Where such a public does not exist, Deliberative Polling provides a way to find out what those concerns might be.

If an experiment is meant to contribute to the public dialogue, its success would require that someone pay attention. At the time of this writing, a Lexis/Nexis search of current news on the National Issues Convention or Deliberative Polling turned up 548 news items.[24] Of these, about fifty focused on the electric utility Deliberative Polls conducted since the NIC (see Section 5 below). Almost all the rest of the items were discussions of the NIC, references to it in light of later developments in the campaign, or references to it in light of attempts by news organizations to replicate the process. The *Minnesota Star Tribune* attempted a full-scale replication on the state level in March 1996 on the issues in the presidential campaign, and the *Portland Press Herald* replicated with a smaller sample "Deliberative Poll" from the town of Sanford, Maine; the poll met throughout the presidential campaign. There were also other efforts to recreate the same kind of citizen dialogue (and which claimed to have been inspired by the NIC), but which lacked the rigor of a scientific random sample.[25] If we include these efforts, but set aside the utility polls, there were nearly five hundred articles generated by the NIC around the country.

This substantial interest reflected the fact that this was a chance to see and hear the public—in microcosm—coming to terms with the issues. The press could, in effect, see "America in one room" telling us all what was on its mind when it began to talk about politics in its own terms—in ways that connect with the concerns of ordinary people.

The NIC combined the richness of a focus group or an issues forum with the statistical representativeness of a national random sample. Instead of only numbers to demonstrate aggregate change, the experiment had the faces of real people—humanizing coverage of the process. This provided unique opportunities both for the television documentary (editing accounts of the small group discussions for the ninety-minute wrap-up broadcast) and for print journalists covering the small group discussions.

A separate analysis of this media coverage is planned.[26] In the meantime, it is worth noting that an experiment measuring the effects of viewing the NIC broadcast and of receiving its briefing materials has shown that the project produced a statistically significant rise in the sense of civic engagement for viewers and readers at home—a rise in the sense of whether respondents in this separate experiment felt that they have a say in government or a decrease in their sense that politicians are out of touch.[27]

One potential benefit of the small group discussions was a better sense of mutual understanding, one that went beyond the stereotypes fostered by television sound bites. For example, at the beginning of one small group discussion on the family, an eighty-four-year-old conservative from Arizona expressed the view that "a family" required that there be both a mother and a father in the home. After three days of dialogue in a group that included a forty-one-year-old woman who had raised two children as a single parent, the Arizonan came up to her at the end of the weekend and asked her what the three words in the English language are that "can define a person's character." He answered his own question with the three words—"I was wrong." "At that, the mother of two got out of her chair, crossed the room and hugged him."[28] A dialogue of several days over the contested meaning of "family" permitted people from different backgrounds to come to a degree of understanding that overcame the simplified stereotypes of media discussion. When the media covers such dialogues, it has an occasion to overcome some of its own limitations.

4. WHAT DID IT MEAN?

Anyone who really listened to the NIC heard the people's agenda—an agenda that inserted itself insistently into the primary process that followed but that was far from clear at the time. For example, one journalist writing from the event, Michael Tackett of the *Chicago Tribune,* summarized the small group discussions by noting this consensus: "They seemed to concur that the most profound problem facing the country is one that most politicians don't seem to talk much about: a growing sense of economic anxiety."[29] Pat Buchanan capitalized on this anxiety as the primary season developed, but it was elusive enough, even one month after the NIC, to surprise Senator Bob Dole. On the eve of the New Hampshire primary he said, "I didn't realize that jobs and trade and what makes America work would become a big issue in the last days of this campaign." He would have heard these concerns clearly had he attended the National Issues Convention in January.

The focus on jobs and the economy, which came to dominate the campaign, could be seen from major shifts in opinion measured in the Deliberative Poll. At the end of the weekend's discussions, there was a sixteen-point increase in the percentage of those who agreed that "today the average worker does not receive a fair day's pay for a fair day's work" (a shift from 59 to 75 percent) and there was a fifteen-point increase in the percentage in those who felt that the "biggest problem for the American family" was "economic pressures" rather than "the breakdown of traditional American values" (from 36 to 51 percent). And while the sample showed no change in opinion on the North American Free Trade Agreement (it was split both before and after), it connected the trade issue to the focus on job insecurity. There was a thirteen-point increase in the percentage of those who agreed that "low trade barriers mean that American jobs will be lost to other countries" (from 55 to 68 percent).

It is also arguable that the participants did not merely identify a problem, but also identified some reasonable first steps about what should be done about it. One striking change was the movement in favor of more investment in education and training (there was a fourteen-point increase to 86 percent in those who thought we spend too little on education and training). Participants were also more concerned with savings and investment than with any program of massive redistribution of wealth. For example, there was a seventeen-point increase (from 66 to 83 percent) in the percentage of those who wanted a "tax break for saving," but there was support for only modest redistribution, despite the concern with stagnating incomes and jobs (only 22 percent, down from 27.5 percent in the "before" poll, thought that those with high incomes should pay a much larger percentage of their income in taxes than should those with low incomes). The sample's views, not very different from those of many experts, seemed to be that incentives for saving along with more investment in education and training would provide, over the long term, an approach to solving their economic difficulties.

In another change that prefigured the dialogue of the campaign, support for the flat tax went flat. The sample came in with 43 percent supporting the flat tax, but this fell to 30 percent after the weekend's discussions. The change was accompanied by an increase in the percentage who were undecided (a rise from 13 to 20 percent), the only item for which "undecideds" increased. The flat tax sounded simple and appealing at first, but many people became less sure once they confronted its complexities.

The Deliberative Poll was not meant to predict public opinion. It was an experiment representing the country in microcosm under conditions where citizens could become more informed and have a real chance to discuss the issues. But as *Adweek* noted in an article about the convention, the experiment constituted a kind of "Focus Group USA"[30]—a serious discussion with the depth of a focus group but with the statistical representativeness of a national random sample. By combining scientific sampling with the personal engagement of focus groups, we created a new entrant to the public dialogue: the televised Deliberative Poll. The result is a "poll with a human face"—real people who express their concerns in terms that make sense to them, but who collectively constitute a microcosm of the entire country.

Conventional focus groups are too small to be statistically representative, and they do not move the discussion very far. They are meant to uncover the views and feelings that people actually have. The discussion groups at the National Issues Convention went a step further by giving people more information and more opportunities to have a dialogue with candidates, experts, and each other. Our participants were empowered to behave more like ideal citizens. Of course, it is questionable whether the actual campaign process offers anything comparable—whether it offers a real chance for people to become more informed or more engaged with the issues. Nevertheless, there is striking overlap between the shifts at the convention and the priorities of the public that became known as the campaign proceeded.

There were also some significant shifts that were not reflected in the campaign. For example, a quarter of the sample, like the country as a whole in other studies, thought that foreign aid was the largest portion of the federal budget. After the deliberative weekend, in which the tiny share of expenditures devoted to foreign aid was made clear (it is close to 1 percent of the budget, depending on how it is defined), respondents no longer wished to get rid of it. Support for maintaining foreign aid at its present level went from 26 percent to 41 percent.

If the Deliberative Poll were to become a regular part of our national life, politicians and policy makers would have to anticipate how their positions would be received, not just in the public's impressions of sound bites in a conventional poll, but in the public's considered judgments after receiving more information. Recent studies show that two-thirds of the public think that we spend more on foreign aid than on Medicare. When Pat Buchanan was asked during the campaign how to balance the budget, he replied that we should protect Medicare but cut foreign aid. Such a proposal might look good to an uninformed public, but it would not have fared well with the informed participants in the Deliberative Poll. They would know that foreign aid is too tiny an expenditure to offer a strategy for balancing the budget and they would have made that clear in a nationally televised event.

Critics have argued that the "Hawthorne effect" vitiates this experiment because the respondents are put in an artificial environment in which they are aware that the media is observing their discussions. The Hawthorne effect comes from research in the 1920s in the Hawthorne Works factory in which the self-consciousness of workers about being part of an experiment changed their behavior. More specifically, it seemed to make them more effective workers.[31] There are several responses to this criticism of the NIC. First, the experimental environment is not as artificial as one might imagine because a major part of the design takes account of the fact that for several weeks before the event the respondents will pay attention to the media, read the briefing materials, and talk with family and friends in order to prepare for the event—all in their natural environment. Second, the environment during the convention is artificial only because the participants are being given, within a short period of time, a good opportunity to get information, to hear opposing points of view, to discuss the issues in an atmosphere of mutual respect with trained moderators, and to come to an informed judgment that they can register in a confidential questionnaire at the end of the proceedings. The elements that make the process in some sense artificial are precisely the elements that improve the quality of deliberation. Because the object of the experiment is to get a picture of public opinion as it might arise if there were high-quality deliberation, the charge of artificiality is really beside the point. Third, the Hawthorne effect arose from studies of workers who became more productive precisely because they were being observed. One of our goals was to see what citizens might be like in conditions where people can behave like more productive citizens. If we can establish an atmosphere of civility and substance in which citizens have every incentive to discuss the issues, then the experiment will have succeeded. The many media accounts of the small group deliberations only confirm that this aspect of the experiment was fully realized. By establishing conditions under which media coverage would be seen as an indication that the views of ordinary citizens are taken seriously, we harnessed the power of the media to a constructive purpose—creating a more seriously engaged and thoughtful public dialogue.

Plans are underway for more Deliberative Polls, both at the national level on policy issues and in future elections, and at the state and local levels, where transportation costs are far less. Television and public opinion polling have given us a superficial form of mass democracy. The public demands more substance than it can get from shrinking sound bites, negative ads, staged photo opportunities, and "debates" that often have the character of food fights. Our respondents, when gathered in Austin, expressed surprise that they could actually "talk politics" without "insulting each other." Those who are seeking their votes might well learn from their example.

5. THE 1997 BRITISH GENERAL ELECTION

I first proposed Deliberative Polling as an opportunity for a representative microcosm to make recommendations to the country on national television in an electoral process. My original interest was the American presidential primary system. As things turned out, the NIC focused on the issues in the presidential campaign, but the deliberative weekend did not include voting intention. However, the aspiration to do a national broadcast that included voting intentions among the questions was finally realized in Britain in a broadcast preceding the 1997 General Election.

As we developed our plans, Channel 4 hosted a symposium in London to brief journalists, pollsters, and academics about the experience.[32] Robert Worcester, head of MORI (Market and Opinion Research International) and other prominent pollsters and commentators expressed some reservations: a) there were unlikely to be any changes in voting intention, b) if there were any changes they would result in "churn"—movements in one direction that would cancel out movements in the other, c) if we focused on positive and substantive arguments rather than negative sound bites, we would be even less likely to get any significant changes, and d) anything revealed on the weekend would have little relevance to the actual election results because the environment we were creating was so artificial.

Fortunately, all four criticisms were misplaced. The experiment produced significant changes in opinion, even in voting intention. These changes were not simply churn, but aggregate differences, before and after the weekend (see Appendix D). Furthermore, these changes occurred despite a consistent effort to keep the discussions with experts and politicians in the plenary sessions focused on positive arguments about the substantive positions of each party. Sheena MacDonald, the presenter of the program, enforced this effort with grace and skill. Lastly, the results offered much insight into the General Election.

In our statements to the press after the weekend but before the election, we emphasized that: "This poll should not be viewed as a prediction but a 'what if'—What if voters had a chance to really get good information and have a sustained and balanced dialogue about the issues in the election? Whom would they support?" Yet we also pointed out that the poll results suggested "a decisive win for Labour, a collapse of Tory support, and a surprising willingness to support the Liberal Democrats."[33] This was, in fact, basically what happened in the General Election. But the percentages in our "after" poll differed from the election percentages, most obviously because our weekend participants moved dramatically toward the Liberal Democrats. The Liberal Democrat percentage went from 11 percent to 33 percent on the weekend, a far larger increase than anyone could realistically expect on a national basis and one that would, by itself, skew the percentages for the other two main parties.

Yet the basic message remained. Our weekend results suggested a Tory collapse. In fact, the Tories got their lowest share of the vote for this century. Our weekend results suggested a resounding Labour win—a result certainly confirmed on Election Day. Our weekend results also suggested a big increase in support for the Liberal Democrats. In fact, the Liberal Democrats got the highest number of seats for a third party since 1929. Commentators were surprised that in key seats where they were competitive, the Liberal Democrats achieved increases as high as twenty points.[34]

The Liberal Democrats concentrated their campaign spending on only fifty seats. Hence decisions to vote for them were complicated by "wasted vote" arguments and tactical voting in each constituency. Nevertheless, it might be argued that the reservoir of support for them suggested by the Deliberative Poll received some confirmation by their increase in seats. This breakthrough was so surprising that the press reported fortunes being made on bets for every seat above twenty-six achieved by the Liberal Democrats.[35]

Not only did the weekend sample increase its support for the Liberal Democrats, it also increased its movement toward specific Liberal Democrat policy positions—on Europe, on taxation, and on investment in education. Our sample became more informed on the issues, more informed on the positions of all three parties on those issues, and more clearly able to connect policy preferences with an evaluation of the parties.

Our participants, of course, had the chance to become more engaged in the political dialogue and more knowledgeable about politics than the rest of the population. In that sense our experiment was intended to set an example for how public consultation in a democracy could work. When the general public also becomes more engaged and more knowledgeable, the Deliberative Poll would seem likely to identify actual opinion changes in the electorate. The general public, however, will often remain ill-informed and inattentive and very different from our microcosm. Hence results on the weekend that differ from those of the election are very much to be expected.

The deliberative weekend also sheds light on the election postmortems. For instance, Chancellor Kenneth Clarke said on election night that if there had only been more discussion of the economy and less discussion of side issues, the Tories might have won. "There was far too little about the economy. If we had less on Europe and a lot less on sleaze we might have done it," he told the BBC.[36] On the other hand, Clarke's critics have said that if only he had not blocked a more clearly defined Eurosceptic's position for the party, the Conservatives might have won. These two speculations highlight the two major weapons thought to be in the Tory arsenal during the campaign—the "boom" (in the slogan "Britain is booming") and "Europe." The deliberative weekend shows how both weapons misfired.

Our sample spent the entire weekend discussing the economy, with carefully balanced briefings, expert input from competing perspectives, and the participation of politicians, including Clarke. After extensive discussions of inflation, unemployment, taxes, and spending, our sample did not increase its support for the Conservatives. In fact, there was an increase from 47 percent to 56 percent in those who "feared for the future" if the Conservatives won the election. After the weekend, only 11 percent (essentially the same as at the start) thought that the economy was "getting a lot stronger."

The weekend sample of 276 broke into fifteen small groups for detailed discussions. One of the groups wrote on the blackboard, "If Britain is booming, where's the money?" Under that they wrote one of their proposed questions for the experts, "Are the unemployment numbers fiddled?" In fact, there is a controversy about how Britain's unemployment numbers are calculated. By standard international criteria, Britain's unemployment rate may be nearly twice what was commonly stated in the campaign.[37] And the "boom" is not yet apparent. There was too much anxiety expressed in the small groups about corporate downsizing, job insecurity, and wages keeping up for many people to actually feel the "feel good" factor.

Similarly, there was greater support for European integration after discussion. Before the weekend, only 36 percent supported uniting fully with Europe. After the weekend's discussions, the percentage increased to 49 percent. And the percentage of people concerned that a single currency would lead Britain to "lose too much control over its own economic policy" fell from 69 to 58 percent. After discussion, strong Euroscepticism was much less a vote winner than many had speculated. This result replicated the basic pattern of a separate Deliberative Poll that we conducted in 1995 on "Britain's Future in Europe" (see Appendix D).

The Deliberative Poll offered a picture of the country making up its mind on the basis of good information. People brought their life experiences to an economic debate in which they were able to compare their perceptions to the claims of competing experts and politicians. Their perceptions of wages, job insecurity, and unemployment led them to process Tory claims for the economy in quite a different manner from the sound bite campaign. On Europe they showed a willingness to moderate their views after discussion—a pattern that has real implications for the continuing battle between Eurosceptics and Europhiles in the Tory party and in Britain as a whole.

This deliberative weekend demonstrated how television can be used to connect voters to the issues and viewers to the campaign. The broadcast reframed the issues in voter's terms, and was an attempt to bring the people into the process in a representative and thoughtful way. The considered judgments of a representative sample were broadcast to the whole country on the weekend before the nation was to make its decision. Television provided a glimpse of a more substantive and balanced campaign process—a glimpse that might help future research and reform efforts.

6. OTHER APPLICATIONS: THE DELIBERATIVE POLL COMES HOME TO LOCAL COMMUNITIES

One of the more unexpected applications for the process came with three local Deliberative Polls on electric utility issues in the summer of 1996. Regulated public utilities in Texas, like those in many other states, are required to consult the public as part of their integrated resource planning—planning for how to provide power for customers in their service territories and for how to deal with the environmental and other tradeoffs that are part of those decisions. The broadcast of America's first Deliberative Poll stimulated interest in adapting the process to utility issues. Traditionally, the utility conducts a standard poll, holds town meetings, or conducts focus groups. The difficulty is that standard polls reveal only that the public has little interest in or information about electric utility matters. Hence polls are likely to report "top of the

head" responses or even "nonattitudes" or nonexistent pseudo-opinions.[38] Town meetings are likely to attract organized interests and lob-
byists rather than the unorganized mass public. And focus groups are
too small ever to be demonstrably representative of the population.
Hence the attraction of Deliberative Polling—it represents the entire
population under conditions where it can get good information and become engaged in the issues.

The three utility polls were conducted with the active cooperation of
stakeholder groups representing environmental issues and consumer
interests, as well as advocates of alternative energy sources. In cooperation with the utility, these stakeholder groups approved all the briefing
materials, the questionnaire, the panels of experts, and the other plans
for the weekend.[39] Representatives from the Public Utility Commission
of Texas participated in all the events, answering questions from the
sample.

Several points should be noted about this application of Deliberative
Polling. First, local versions of the process are far more cost effective
because respondents do not need to be transported over an entire country. Second, the process brought the people into an actual policymak-
ing process—allowing them to decide how to provide electric power for
the regions in question. The recommendations of the people were
scrupulously followed by the utilities, not only in the judgment of the
utilities, but also in the judgment and public statement of relevant
stakeholders.[40] Third, the Public Utility Commission reacted to participation in the process by changing its rules to require that the public be
consulted only after it has been informed on the issues. It adopted new
rules in July 1996, specifying that public participation had to be statistically representative of customers, that there must be a two-way
process of dialogue, that participants in the dialogue had to receive ac-
curate and balanced information representing competing viewpoints,
and that quantitative assessment of their concluding views should be
reported as part of the process. While these requirements do not specify Deliberative Polling, it should be clear that either Deliberative

Polling or similar methods will now become part of the actual policy process in the state.

The three utility polls, all conducted within a short period of time, should also set to rest two areas of debate about Deliberative Polling. First, some have questioned whether the Deliberative Poll produces large changes of opinion. The answer probably depends on the issue. The utility polls highlight the fact that on issues where the public has not invested a lot of time and attention, the changes are likely to be large because the public is arriving at a considered judgment where previous responses would have represented only "top of the head" views or even "nonattitudes" or nonexistent opinions. For example, in the utility polls respondents were asked to specify the "first choice" energy option from four possibilities—renewable energy such as wind or solar power, fossil fuel plants such as gas or coal, investment in conservation to reduce energy needs, or buying and transporting energy from outside the service territory. The three Deliberative Polls all exhibited the same pattern: renewable energy, as the first choice, fell from 67 to 16 percent at Central Power and Light (CPL); from 35 percent at West Texas Utilities (WTU); and from 67 to 28 percent at Southwest Electric Power (SWEPCO). These are all massive changes in opinion. Furthermore, the recurrence of the pattern offers a response to a second issue. Some critics have argued that Deliberative Polls should be considered unique events that cannot be replicated. The three utility polls, however, held in different service territories, with different samples, with different expert panels, but with similar briefings revealed a remarkably similar dynamic all three times.[41] First, there was the large drop, already noted, in support for renewable energy as a first choice. Respondents were interested in renewable energy, but once they learned the complexities of wind mills or solar power as the principal power supply, their response was to sharply increase their support for conservation. Conservation implements some of the same environmental values as renewable energy and, they learned, was cost effective. Hence, support for conservation as the first choice rose from 11 to

46 percent at CPL, from 7 to 31 percent at WTU, and from 16 to 50 percent at SWEPCO. The respondents did not abandon their interest in renewable energy, however. They just came to see it as an essential part of the mix—one they were willing to pay extra for to implement. The percentage of the respondents willing to pay at least $1 more on their monthly bill for renewable energy rose from 58 to 81 percent at CPL, from 56 to 90 percent at WTU, and from 52 to 84 percent at SWEPCO. Therefore, the basic dynamic of opinion change was replicated three times in a row.

The Deliberative Poll was modeled after ancient Athenian democracy, where randomly selected microcosms were part of local government decision-making. After 2,400 years, this kind of democracy returned to local decision-making—in this case electric utility service territories. We are only beginning to explore the possibilities for informed statistical microcosms as an input to the policy process and to the political process. But the hope is that in an age of pseudo-public voices, of spin doctors, attack ads, self-selected polls, and staged town meetings, the Deliberative Poll can provide a useful insight into public opinion and a useful input into public decision processes.

APPENDIX A

The First Deliberative Poll:
Summary of Results

At this writing, I am at work with my academic colleagues in the British Deliberative Poll—Robert Luskin (University of Texas) and Roger Jowell and Rebecca Gray (both of SCPR) on a systematic analysis of what happened in the Manchester deliberative poll of 1994. We have joint publications in preparation. In the meantime, this informal summary may provide a useful picture of the experiment.

REPRESENTATIVENESS

The independent London research institute SCPR selected a national random sample from forty randomly chosen polling districts in forty randomly chosen constituencies in Great Britain. Of this sample, 869 people responded to a baseline survey, with a response rate of 74 percent. Three hundred people participated in the Manchester experiment, held April 15–17, 1994. On every demographic and attitudinal dimension, the 300 are indistinguishable from the 869.

On the issue of whether crime is a worry, for example, note this comparison of the baseline survey and the weekend sample:

Crime	Baseline survey	Weekend sample
No worry	28%	27%
A big worry	22%	21%
A bit of a worry	34%	35%
An occasional doubt	16%	17%

Furthermore, on every important question about what should be done about crime, the weekend sample presented a near-perfect microcosm of the baseline sample. To take just two key ways of reducing crime, "reducing unemployment" and giving "stiffer sentences generally," the following results were discovered:

	Very effective	Effective	Neither effective nor ineffective	Not very effective	Not at all effective
Reduce unemployment					
Total	43	38	7	9	3
Weekend	44	38	11	4	3
Stiffer sentences generally					
Total	52	26	13	6	3
Weekend	51	27	15	5	2

RESULTS: BEFORE AND AFTER

Key changes in the After survey (compared to the baseline survey for the three hundred):

1. The respondents show an increased sense of the limitations of prison as a tool for fighting crime.
   •Agree that "send more offenders to prison" is an effective way of preventing crime: down from 57 to 38 percent (**).

•Agree that "the courts should send fewer people to prison": up from 29 to 44 percent (**).

•Agree that "stiffer sentences generally" is an effective way of fighting crime: down from 78 to 65 percent (**).

2. The respondents show an increased willingness to employ alternatives to prison, both for juveniles and for offenders more generally.

•Strongly against sending first-time burglar, aged 16, to an ordinary prison: up from 33 to 50 percent (**).

•Agree to a strict warning while leaving the juvenile to the parents to sort out: up from 49 to 63 percent (**).

•Favor compulsory training and counseling for criminals who are not a big threat to society: up from 66 to 75 percent (**).

•"If the government had to choose, it should concentrate more on punishing criminals or it should concentrate more on trying to reform criminals": punish, down from 54 to 47 percent (*).

3. The responses show an increased sensitivity to procedural rights of defendants.

•Strongly disagree that the police should sometimes be able to "bend the rules" to get a conviction: up from 37 to 46 percent (**).

•Believe it is "worse to convict an innocent person" than "to let a guilty person go free": up from 62 to 70 percent (**).

•Agree that "suspects should have the right to remain silent under police questioning": up from 36 to 50 percent (**).

•Agree that "if a suspect remains silent under police questioning this should count against them in court": down from 58 to 41 percent (**).

•Agree that "a confession made during police questioning should not on its own be enough to convict someone": up from 67 to 78 percent (**).

4. In spite of the increased sensitivity to procedural rights, the respondents remain tough on crime. They have *not* been turned into "lib-

erals": they remain impatient with the impediments to getting a conviction.

•Agree that "the rules in court should be *less* on the side of the accused": up from 42 to 52 percent (**).

•Agree that "the death penalty is the most appropriate sentence" for some crimes: unchanged at 68 percent.

•Agree that "prison life should be made tougher and more unpleasant": unchanged at 71 percent.

•Agree that "Prison life is too soft": virtually unchanged at 75 from 73 percent.

5. The respondents also show movement toward traditional values.

•Agree that "teach children the difference between right and wrong" is a very effective way to help prevent crime: up from 66 to 77 percent (**).

•Agree that "parents spending more time with their children" is a very effective way to help prevent crime: up from 53 to 66 percent (**).

•Agree that "less violence and crime on television" is an effective way of preventing crime: up from 67 to 74 percent (**).

6. Respondents show increased knowledge on issue of crime.

•"Britain has a larger prison population than any other country in Western Europe": correct (true), up from 50 to 80 percent (**).

•"Britain has more people serving life sentences than the rest of the European Community put together": correct (true), up from 20 to 58 percent (**).

•"Possible to be tried by a jury in a local magistrate's court": correct (false), up from 58 to 68 percent (**).

Note that all the changes above are *net change*. Many more respondents changed than is indicated by these figures because on many questions change in one direction was canceled out by change in the other. For example, on "the courts should treat suspects as innocent until proved guilty" there was virtually no net change, but only half (46 percent) gave the same answer both times.

Note: The symbol (*) means that the difference between the before and after survey is significant at the 5 percent level in a two-tailed test, and (**) that the difference is significant at 1 percent level.

APPENDIX B

Who Came?

Some Comparisons of Weekend Sample

to Entire Baseline Survey (in Percentages)

	Baseline	Weekend
Race		
White	80	78
Black	12	13
Hispanic	6	7
Gender		
Male	46	47
Female	54	53
Age		
18–29	21	24
30–39	26	29
40–49	18	20
50–59	13	13
60–69	11	9
70+	11	5
Religion		
Protestant	46	45
Catholic	32	32
Jewish	2	2

(continued)

	Baseline	Weekend
Religion		
Muslim	1	1
None	4	5
Other	15	15
Party affiliation		
Republican	31	32
Democrat	34	34
Independent	26	26
1992 vote		
Clinton	46	46
Bush	37	35
Perot	17	19
Frequency with which respondent watches news		
Never	3	3
Less than once a month	3	4
Once a month	3	2
Several times a month	4	4
Once a week	9	8
Several times a week	27	31
Every day	51	49
Frequency with which respondent works for political campaigns		
Most elections	2	2
Some elections	7	9
A few elections	13	15
Never	79	74
Frequency with which respondent talks to others about politics		
Nearly every day	23	27
Once a week	37	43
Once a month	17	15
Less than once a month	23	15

APPENDIX C

Comparison of Sample Delegates
with U.S. Census Data

	U.S. population: 18 and over	Sample delegates
Median income		
Household	$22,240	
Family	$36,749	$30,000–34,999
Unrelated individual	$15,190	
Gender		
Men	48%	48%
Women	52%	52%
Race/Ethnicity		
White	77%	78%
African-American	11%	13%
Hispanic	8%	7%
Other	4%	3%
Age		
Average (Years)	44.25	41.27

(continued)

	U.S. population: 18 and over	Sample delegates
Distribution		
18–29	23.5%	24%
30–39	23.4%	29%
40–49	18.5%	20%
50–59	12.5%	13%
60–69	10.9%	9%
70+	11.2%	5%
Education		
No high school diploma	20.0%	10.9%
High school graduates	34.8%	34.3%
Some college	25.2%	27.4%
College degree and above	20.0%	27.4%
Region		
Northeast	20.5%	18.6%
Midwest	23.7%	22.7%
South	34.4%	30.3%
West	21.3%	28.4%

Source: NORC and Current Population Survey of the Bureau of the Census, March 1993.

APPENDIX D

Eight Deliberative Polls, 1994–97:
How Participants Change (Selected Results)

THE NATIONAL ISSUES CONVENTION,
JANUARY 1996, AUSTIN, TEXAS

	Before Deliberation (percentage)	After Deliberation (percentage)	Difference (percentage)
In favor of:			
"A tax reduction for savings"	66	83	+17
"Flat tax"	44	30	−14
"Education and training" (agree that we are now spending "too little")	72	86	+14
"Foreign aid" (agree that current level is "about right")	26	41	+15
"Safety net for welfare and health care" should be turned over to the states "to decide how much to give"	50	63	+13

(continued)

	Before Deliberation (percentage)	After Deliberation (percentage)	Difference (percentage)
In favor of:			
"Making divorce harder to get" (as a way of strengthening the family)	36	57	+21
"Military cooperation with other nations to address trouble spots in the world" ("agree strongly that U.S. should continue")	21	38	+17
"Biggest problem facing the American family" is "economic pressure"	36	51	+15
"Biggest problem facing the American family" is "breakdown of traditional values"	58	48	−10

BRITISH DELIBERATIVE POLL ON CRIME, 1994

	Before Deliberation (percentage)	After Deliberation (percentage)	Difference (percentage)
Agree that:			
"Sending more offenders to prison" is "an effective way of fighting crime"	57	38	−19
"The rules in court should be LESS on the side of the accused"	42	52	+10

(continued)

BRITISH DELIBERATIVE POLL ON CRIME (CONTINUED)

	Before Deliberation (percentage)	After Deliberation (percentage)	Difference (percentage)
Agree that:			
"Suspects should have the right to remain silent under police questioning"	36	50	+14
Disagree that:			
"The police should sometimes be able to 'bend the rules' to get a conviction" (strongly disagree)	37	46	+ 9
"First time burglar, age 16," should be sent to an ordinary prison (strongly disagree)	33	50	+17

BRITISH DELIBERATIVE POLL ON EUROPE, 1995

	Before Deliberation (percentage)	After Deliberation (percentage)	Difference (percentage)
Agree that:			
Britain is a lot better off in the EU than out of it	45	60	+15
Closer links with EU would make Britain stronger economically	51	67	+16
If we left EU Britain would lose its best chance of real progress	40	53	+13

(continued)

	Before Deliberation (percentage)	After Deliberation (percentage)	Difference (percentage)
Agree that:			
With single currency, Britain would lose control of its own economic policy	62	50	−12

BRITISH DELIBERATIVE POLL ON THE MONARCHY, 1996

	Before Deliberation (percentage)	After Deliberation (percentage)	Difference (percentage)
Agree that:			
"The Monarchy makes me proud to be British"	48	59	+11
"The Monarchy's role in uniting people from throughout Britain" is "very important"	32	41	+ 9
"The Monarchy should remain as it is"	51	39	−12
"The Monarchy should be reformed"	34	50	+16
The "Monarch should not stay head of the Church of England"	26	56	+30

1997 DELIBERATIVE POLL IN THE
BRITISH GENERAL ELECTION

A national random sample was drawn from ninety constituencies in England, Scotland, and Wales. The 276 weekend participants were drawn from a baseline poll conducted in January of 1,210 respondents with a response rate of 64 percent of the named participants drawn from the electoral register. The representativeness of the weekend group was supported by comparisons of its attitudes and demographics to the entire baseline poll and to other polls as well as to Census data. The weekend dialogue included discussions with the three candidates for chancellor—Kenneth Clarke (Conservative), Gordon Brown (Labour), and Malcolm Bruce (Liberal Democrat). There were also two panels of experts who answered questions from the sample. The panels had one expert each connected with one of the parties, plus an independent expert. The survey research was conducted by Social and Community Planning Research (SCPR), an independent research institute based in London. The results were broadcast nationally on Channel 4 for two hours at the conclusion of the weekend, Sunday evening, April 28, 1997.

VOTING INTENTION (IN PERCENTAGES)

	Before weekend	After weekend
Conservative	26	19
Labour	47	39
Liberal Democrat	11	33
Scottish National	1	1
Plaid Cymru	1	1
Another party	3	3
Would not vote	3	1
Can't choose	7	5
Not answered	0	2

	Before weekend	After weekend
Agree that people earning about 50,000 pounds a year or more should pay higher income tax.		
Agree or agree strongly	66%	81%
Agree that government should do more to unite fully with European Union.		
	36%	49%
Agree that government should unite fully with European Union (identified as Liberal Democrat view).		
	46%	62%
Unless Britain keeps its own currency, it will lose too much control over its own economic policy.		
Agree or strongly agree	69%	48%
I fear for the future of Britain if the Conservative Party wins the general election.		
Agree or strongly agree	47%	56%
I fear for the future of Britain if the Labour Party wins the general election.		
Agree or strongly agree	29%	28%
Britain's economy would be much better off if the Liberal Democrats formed part of the next government.		
Agree or strongly agree	42%	51%

As a "post-test only control group" we also commissioned Gallup questions in a separate probability sample at the time of the April broadcast. Other Gallup results also provided a point of comparison in January at the time of recruitment.

	January Gallup	Deliberative Weekend Sample in January	April Gallup	Deliberative Poll (After)
Conservative	27	26	27	19
Labour	44	47	42	39
Lib Dem	8	11	12	33

Under which government would you be economically better off?

	Deliberative Weekend Sample in January	April Gallup	Deliberative Poll (After)
Conservative	27	26	28
Labour	35	34	43

UTILITY POLLS CONDUCTED BY CPL (CENTRAL POWER AND LIGHT), WTU (WEST TEXAS UTILITIES) AND SWEPCO (SOUTH WEST ELECTRIC POWER), 1996

	Before Deliberation (percentage)	After Deliberation (percentage)	Difference (percentage)
Option to pursue first (to provide additional electric power to service territory)			
Renewable energy (CPL)	67	16	−51
Renewable energy (WTU)	71	35	−36
Renewable energy (SWEPCO)	67	28	−39
Invest in conservation (CPL)	11	46	+35
Invest in conservation (WTU)	7	31	+24
Invest in conservation (SWEPCO)	16	50	+34
Build fossil fuel plant (CPL)	11	29	+18
Buy and transport power (WTU)	10	18	+ 8
Percentage of customers who were willing to pay *at least* $1 more on their monthly bill for renewable energy			
CPL	58	81	+23
WTU	56	90	+34
SWEPCO	52	84	+32

APPENDIX E

Do the Changes Last?

British Deliberative Poll on Crime

	Round 1 (at recruitment) (percentage)	Round 2 (end of weekend) (percentage)	Round 3 (10 months after) (percentage)
Send more offenders to prison			
	57	38	43
In favor of right to silence			
	36	50	42
Worse to convict innocent than let guilty go free			
	59	70	64
Britain has bigger prison population than anywhere else in Western Europe			
	50	82	72

Note: Respondents were contacted about ten months after the deliberative weekend.

APPENDIX F

How Participants Evaluated
the Process at the NIC

These questions were added to the final questionnaire administered at the end of the weekend.

37. Overall, for me the National Issues Convention was . . .

%	.2	0	.5	.7	2.1	2.5	8.1	12.7	73.3%
	1	2	3	4	5	6	7	8	9

Generally a   An extremely
waste of time   valuable experience

38. How valuable in helping you clarify your positions on the issues were each of the different parts of the National Issues Convention listed below?

	Little or no value (1)	Somewhat valuable (2)	Very valuable (3)
a. Participating in the group discussions	1.2%	16.8%	82.0%
b. Meeting and talking to other delegates outside of the group discussions	5.1%	29.7%	65.2%
c. The sessions with the political leaders on TV	13.5%	44.8%	41.8%

39. Please indicate whether you agree or disagree with each of the following statements about the discussion groups.

	Disagree strongly	Disagree	Agree	Agree strongly
a. The group leader provided the opportunity for everyone to participate in the discussion.				
	.9%	0%	20%	79.1%
b. The important aspects of each issue were covered in the group discussions.				
	1.2%	5.4%	39.3%	54.2%
c. I found many of the comments of other group members useful in my thinking about the issues.				
	.9%	4.9%	43.6%	50.6%
d. The group leader often tried to influence the group with his or her views.				
	79.3%	14%	3.7%	3%
e. I discovered that people with views very different from mine often had very good reasons for their views.				
	1.6%	5.3%	52.8%	40.2%

40. Overall, how much did you learn about the presidential candidates' positions on each of the issues you discussed?

A great deal	(1)	27.7%
Some	(2)	47.0%
A little	(3)	20.7%
Almost nothing at all	(4)	4.7%

41. Now think back to the time after you were interviewed in your home but before you came to the convention. During this period how much did you do each of the following activities?

	A little less than usual	About the same as usual	A little more than usual
a. Talked with others about politics			
	11.6%	43.4%	45.0%

	A little less than usual	About the same as usual	A little more than usual
b. Read about politics in newspapers and magazines			
	9.5%	45.3%	45.1%
c. Watched the network news or other public affairs programs on television	8.6%	49.9%	41.5%

42. During that time period, about how much time did you spend reading the discussion materials that were sent to you?

Just glanced at the material	(1)	13.7%
Read less than half of the materials	(2)	5.6%
Read about half of the materials	(3)	11.2%
Read more than half of the materials	(4)	15.6%
Read most or all of the materials	(5)	54.0%

43. Did you think the discussion materials were mostly balanced, or that they clearly favored some positions over others?

Mostly balanced	(1)	80.8%
Favored some positions over others	(2)	15.7%
Don't know	(3)	3.5%

44. As you know, the three issues chosen for discussion at the National Issues convention were America's global role, the economy, and family values. Do you think these were the right issues to discuss at the convention, or do you think that there are some more important issues that should have been included?

Issues chosen were the right ones	(1)	68.5%
Other issues should have been discussed	(2)	28.3%
Don't know	(3)	3.2%

APPENDIX G

National Issues Convention Committees
and Advisory Board

There were three committees that played key roles in the National Issues Convention. The briefing materials were reviewed for accuracy and balance by the Review Committee. The survey research, sample selection, and questionnaire design were overseen by the Technical Review Committee. The entire project was conducted under the auspices of a national advisory board. The members of these committees are listed below. The project was cosponsored by all eleven of the nation's presidential libraries, PBS, and the University of Texas at Austin with support from Freddie Mac, the Annie E. Casey Foundation, Southwestern Bell, American Airlines, the Kettering Foundation, the National Issues Forums, Public Agenda, the city of Austin, and numerous others. Charls E. Walker, senior adviser to the project and co-chair of the National Issues Convention Advisory Board, played a crucial role in every aspect of the project.

REVIEW COMMITTEE

William Frenzel (co-chair)
Guest Scholar in Governmental Studies, The Brookings Institution;
Former Republican Congressman, Minnesota

Barbara Jordan (co-chair)
Lyndon Baines Johnson Centennial Chair in National Policy, LBJ
School, University of Texas at Austin; Former Democratic
Congresswoman, Texas

David L. Boren
President, University of Oklahoma; Former Governor, State of
Oklahoma; Former Democratic Senator, Oklahoma

Bill E. Brock
President, The Brock Group; Former Republican Senator, Tennessee;
Former Chairman, Republican National Committee

Thomas J. Downey
President, Downey, Chandler, Inc.; Former Democratic
Congressman, New York

Kenneth M. Duberstein
Chairman and CEO, The Duberstein Group; Former Chief of Staff to
President Reagan

William A. Galston
Professor, School of Public Affairs, University of Maryland at
College Park; Director, Institute for Philosophy and Public Policy;
Former Deputy Assistant to President Clinton for Domestic Policy

William H. Gray III
President and CEO, United Negro College Fund; Former Democratic
Congressman, Pennsylvania

Robert H. Michel
Senior Advisor, Corporate & Governmental Affairs, Hogan & Hartson, L.L.P.; Former Republican Congressman, Illinois; Former House Republican Leader

Vin Weber
Partner, Clark & Weinstock, Inc.; Former Republican Congressman, Minnesota

NIC TECHNICAL REVIEW COMMITTEE

Phil Converse (Chair), University of Michigan
Norman Bradburn, National Opinion Research Center (NORC)
Henry Brady, University of California, Berkeley
Sheldon Gawiser, Gawiser Associates, Inc.
Jim Davis, NORC
Ken Rasinski, NORC
Andy Kohut, Pew Center
Tom Smith, NORC
Robert Luskin, University of Texas at Austin
Noelle McAfee, University of Texas at Austin
James Fishkin, University of Texas at Austin
Warren Miller, University of Arizona

NATIONAL ISSUES CONVENTION ADVISORY BOARD

The Hon. Newton Minow, Co-chairman
Dr. Charls E. Walker, Co-chairman
The Hon. Toney Anaya
The Hon. Howard H. Baker, Jr.
Dr. Robert M. Berdahl
Mr. Jack S. Blanton

The Hon. John Brademas
Professor Norman Bradburn
The Hon. Bill Brock
Dr. Albert Carnesale
Mr. George Christian
The Hon. William Coleman, Jr.
Professor Philip Converse
The Hon. Lloyd Cutler

Professor Robert Dahl

Mr. Paul Duke

Professor Joel L. Fleishman

The Hon. Henry H. Fowler

The Hon. Bill Frenzel

Ms. Suzanne Garment

General Andrew J. Goodpaster

The Hon. William H. Gray III

Ms. Ellen Hume

The Hon. William Hobby

Admiral B. R. Inman

Professor Shanto Iyengar

Dean Kathleen Hall Jamieson

Professor Barbara Jordan

Mr. Bryce Jordan

Mr. Vernon E. Jordan, Jr.

Ambassador Max M.
    Kampelman

Professor Stanley Kelley, Jr.

Charles A. LeMaistre, M.D.

The Hon. Tom Loeffler

Ambassador Sol M. Linowitz

Mr. Thomas W. Luce II

Dr. Bruce MacLaury

Mr. Thomas E. Mann

The Hon. David Mathews

Mr. David Maxwell

The Hon. Ann D. McLaughlin

Mr. Harry C. McPherson, Jr.

Mr. Bill Moyers

Mr. Robert A. Neuman

Mr. Norman J. Ornstein

Professor Nelson W. Polsby

Mr. Jody Powell

Professor George E. Reedy

Mrs. Sharon Percy Rockefeller

Professor Elspeth Davies
    Rostow

Professor Walt W. Rostow

The Hon. Donald H. Rumsfeld

Professor Larry J. Sabato

The Hon. L. William Seidman

The Hon. Raymond Shafer

The Hon. George P. Shultz

Mr. Hugh Sidey

Mr. Hedrick Smith

Professor Frank Sorauf

Mr. Alexander B. Trowbridge

Mr. Sander Vanocur

The Hon. Paul Volcker

The Hon. Arnold R. Weber

The Hon. Vin Weber

Ms. Anne Wexler

Mr. John C. Whitehead

NOTES

Chapter 1
Introduction

1. There are well-known difficulties with any claim that a particular town or district mirrors the nation. See, for example, Edward R. Tufte and Richard A. Sun, "Are there Bellwether Electoral Districts?" *Public Opinion Quarterly* 39:1 (Spring, 1975): 1–18. Even Tufte and Sun, who see only limited predictive power in bellwether districts, identify 12 counties out of 3,100 that averaged within 2.5 points of the national electoral swing during the period they studied, 1916–1968. As befits the probable location of Grandview, 11 of the 12 are in either north central Illinois or northern Indiana.

2. See Bruce A. Ackerman, "Constitutional Law/Constitutional Politics," *Yale Law Journal* 99 (1989): 453–547, for similar observations.

3. I would like to thank Walter Dean Burnham for his generous help with this discussion of third parties.

4. David Mathews, president of the Kettering Foundation, has made this point eloquently.

5. *The* Republic *of Plato,* trans. Francis MacDonald Cornford (New York: Oxford University Press, 1982), p. 227.

6. See "Fair Exchange," *Newsday,* April 6, 1993, p. 46.

7. I am indebted to Tom Seung for his study of Plato's *Laws.* See T. K. Seung, *Rediscovering Plato* (Lanham, Md.: Rowman and Littlefield, 1996).

8. I take this phrase from Alexander Hamilton, in *Federalist* no. 71. See Hamilton, James Madison, John Jay, *The Federalist Papers,* ed. Clinton Rossiter (New York: New American Library, 1961), p. 432.

9. V. O. Key, Jr. (with Milton Cummings), *The Responsible Electorate* (Cambridge, Mass.: Harvard University Press, 1966), p. 2.

Chapter 2
Who Speaks for the People?

1. Alexander Hamilton, James Madison, John Jay, *The Federalist Papers*, ed. Clinton Rossiter (New York: New American Library, 1961), p. 33. All further references to the *Federalist* will be to this edition and will be cited in text by issue number. See also Herbert J. Storing, ed., *The Complete Anti-Federalist*. 7 vols. (Chicago: University of Chicago Press, 1981), vol. 1, p. 3.

2. Mogens Herman Hansen, *The Athenian Democracy in the Age of Demosthenes* (Oxford: Basil Blackwell, 1991), p. 55.

3. *The Politics of Aristotle,* ed. and trans. Ernest Barker (New York: Oxford University Press, 1958), 1326b, pp. 291–292.

4. As we shall see, "electronic town meetings" will tend to be neither representative nor deliberative. Even the Deliberative Poll (see Chapter 5) does not fulfill mass participation.

5. We now know that there were some 750 city-states in ancient Greece, many of them democracies. But the detailed historical record has restricted most discussion of ancient Greek democracy to Athens.

6. See Clinton Rossiter in Hamilton, Madison, Jay, *Federalist Papers,* p. 100.

7. Anthony Downs, *An Economic Theory of Democracy* (New York: Harper and Row, 1956).

8. See Samuel Popkin, *The Reasoning Voter* (Chicago: University of Chicago Press, 1991).

9. At least, that is the term some modern scholars have used. See Jon Elster, *Solomonic Judgments: Studies in the Limitations of Rationality* (Cambridge: Cambridge University Press, 1989), pp. 85–86. The principal source for the Spartan system is Plutarch's *Lycurgus*. See *Plutarch on Sparta,* trans. Richard A. Talbert (London: Penguin Books, 1988). A detailed description of the Shout can be found on pp. 38–39.

10. Michael Wines, "Washington Really Is in Touch. We're the Problem," *New York Times,* October 16, 1994, sect. 4, p. 1.

11. By engaged citizens, I mean those with incentives to participate in our ideal of democratic discussion.

12. Quoted in "Ears Glued to Phones," *Roll Call,* February 1, 1993.

13. "Rhode Island's Assembly Refuses to Call a Convention and Submits the Constitution Directly to the People," in Bernard Bailyn, ed., *The Debate on the Constitution: Federalist and Antifederalist Speeches, Articles and Letters during the Struggle over Ratification,* Part 2 (New York: Library of America, 1993), pp. 270–275; quotations from p. 274.

14. "The Freemen of Providence Submit Eight Reasons for Calling a Convention, March 26, 1788," in Bailyn, *Debate,* pp. 277–278.

15. North Carolina also turned down the Constitution in a state convention, but after Madison gave notice that he would press Congress for a Bill of Rights, a second

convention, convened at Fayetteville, approved the Constitution in November 1789. See Michael Lienesch, "North Carolina: Preserving Rights," in Michael Allen Gillespie and Michael Lienesch, eds., *Ratifying the Constitution* (Lawrence: University Press of Kansas, 1989), pp. 343–367, esp. pp. 362–364.

16. See John P. Kaminsky, "Rhode Island: Protecting State Interests," in *Ratifying the Constitution*, pp. 368–390.

17. Samuel Greene Arnold, *History of the State of Rhode Island and Providence Plantations,* vol. 1: 1636–1700 (New York: Appleton, 1859), p. 102.

18. Ibid., p. 203.

19. "Speech to the Electors of Bristol on Being Elected (Nov. 1774)" in *The Political Philosophy of Edmund Burke,* ed. Iain Hampsher-Monk (London: Longman, 1987).

20. Ibid., p. 110.

21. *Roll Call,* February 1, 1993.

22. Quoted in Storing, *Complete Anti-Federalist,* vol. 2, p. 379.

23. William C. Adams, "As New Hampshire Goes . . . ," in Gary R. Orren and Nelson W. Polsby, eds., *Media and Momentum: The New Hampshire Primary and Nomination Politics* (Chatham, N.J.: Chatham House, 1987), pp. 42–59. See esp. p. 42.

24. See Adams, pp. 44–45.

25. See, for example, Jürgen Habermas, "A Reply to My Critics," in John B. Thompson and David Held, eds., *Habermas: Critical Debates* (Cambridge, Mass: MIT Press, 1982), pp. 218–283.

26. See the creative proposals by Norman Ornstein and Thomas Mann in *Renewing Congress* (Washington, D.C.: American Enterprise Institute, 1992).

27. Blendon is quoted in "Health-Care Polls Perplex Congress; Debate Leaves the Public Confused," *Chicago Tribune,* May 16, 1994, p. N 7. See also Kaiser Health Reform Project: Kaiser/Harvard/PSRA *Survey of Public Knowledge II* (March 1994), Henry J. Kaiser Family Foundation, Menlo Park, California. A good example of efforts to present Americans with polls that offer trade offs is the work of the Americans Talk Issues Foundation. See Alan F. Kay, Frederick T. Steeper, Hazel Henderson, Celinda Lake, and David J. Hansen, "What the American People Want in the Federal Budget" (Washington, D.C.: Americans Talk Issues Foundation, 1992), Survey 18.

28. See Joseph Tussman, *Obligation and the Body Politic* (New York: Oxford University Press, 1960).

29. Judith N. Shklar, *American Citizenship: The Quest for Inclusion* (Cambridge, Mass.: Harvard University Press, 1991), pp. 25–26.

30. Of course, the United States is unusual for putting the entire burden of registration on the individual citizen. Some have argued that the appropriate comparison is the percentage of registered (rather than eligible) voters who vote. See David Glass, Peveril Squire, and Raymond Wolfinger, "Voter Turnout: An International Comparison," *Public Opinion* 6:6 (December–January 1984): 49–55.

31. See, most notably, Raymond Wolfinger and Steven Rosenstone, *Who Votes?* (New Haven: Yale University Press, 1980).

32. Frances Fox Piven and Richard A. Cloward, *Why Americans Don't Vote* (New York: Pantheon, 1989), p. 12.

33. Maureen Dowd, "Americans Like GOP Agenda but Split on How to Reach Goals," *New York Times,* December 15, 1994, p. 1.

34. Newt Gingrich, interviewed on CNN, January 4, 1994, before the opening session of the new Congress.

35. I am grateful to my colleague Walter Dean Burnham for sharing these perceptive observations with me and for giving me permission to refer to these data.

36. See for example, Steven J. Rosenstone and John Mark Hansen, *Mobilization, Participation and Democracy in America* (New York: Macmillan, 1993), p. 42.

37. *Roll Call,* February 1, 1993.

38. Stephen Engelberg, "A New Breed of Hired Hands Cultivates Grass Roots Anger," *New York Times,* March 17, 1993, sect. A, p. 1.

39. Samuel Butler, *Hudibras,* quoted in Edmund S. Morgan, *Inventing the People: The Rise of Popular Sovereignty in England and America* (New York: Norton, 1988), p. 227.

40. Joseph A. Schumpeter, *Capitalism, Socialism and Democracy* (New York: Harper and Row, 1942), pp. 242–243.

41. I take the term *Constitutional Moment* from Bruce Ackerman. See his *We the People: Foundations* (Cambridge, Mass.: Harvard University Press, 1990).

42. Daniel A. Farber and Suzanna Sherry, *A History of the American Constitution* (Saint Paul, Minn.: West Publishing, 1990), pp. 16–17.

43. For a useful overview see Elmer E. Cornwell, Jr., *Presidential Leadership of Public Opinion* (Bloomington: Indiana University Press, 1965), chap. 2.

44. Push polls are a misuse of survey research for negative campaigning. In a push poll, a misleading characterization of a candidate or position is communicated to the public through widespread telephone pollings.

45. Robert A. Dahl, *A Preface to Democratic Theory* (Chicago: University of Chicago Press, 1956), p. 6. Throughout this book, I am greatly influenced by Dahl's landmark discussion.

46. For a more extended development of this notion of majority tyranny, see my *Tyranny and Legitimacy* (Baltimore: Johns Hopkins University Press, 1979).

47. I wrote this after Proposition 187 in California was passed, in 1994. This proposition, among other things, denies secondary education to the children of illegal immigrants.

48. Hansen, *Athenian Democracy,* pp. 313–314. No citizen could repeat as "president of Athens" after serving for a single day (certainly a most severe version of term limits).

49. See Stanley Crawford, *Mayordomo: Chronicle of an Acequia in Northern New Mexico* (Albuquerque: University of New Mexico Press, 1988).

50. Ralph Waldo Emerson, "Historical Discourse at Concord," quoted in Jane J. Mansbridge, *Beyond Adversary Democracy* (New York: Basic, 1980), p. 126.

51. See Mansbridge, ibid., pp. 130–132.

52. Max Farrand, ed., *The Records of the Federal Convention of 1787*. Rev. ed. 4 vols. (New Haven: Yale University Press, 1966), vol. 1, p. 50.

53. I am indebted to Jane J. Mansbridge for this observation.

54. Stanley Elkins and Eric McKitrick, *The Age of Federalism: The Early American Republic, 1788–1800* (New York: Oxford, 1993), p. 22. Hamilton was more elitist than Madison, and among the Founders there were advocates for greater popular participation. James Wilson of Pennsylvania, for example, argued for popular election of the Senate as well as of the president. He was, in other words, against the Founders' initial strategy of successive filtrations.

55. Quoted in Douglass Adair, *Fame and the Founding Fathers*, ed. Trevor Colbourn (New York: Norton, 1974), pp. 99–100.

56. James Madison, "Vices of the Political System of United States," in Robert A. Rutland et al., eds., *The Papers of James Madison* (Chicago: University of Chicago Press, 1975), p. 357.

57. Storing, *Complete Anti-Federalist*, vol. 2, pp. 380–381.

58. Ibid., vol. 2, p. 249.

59. Ibid., vol. 3, p. 158.

60. Ibid., vol. 1, p. 61.

61. See for example, Storing, ibid., vol. 4, p. 275: "Annual election is the basis of responsibility" ("A Colombian Patriot"), vol. 3, p. 159 (the Pennsylvania Minority objecting to "long terms in office"); and vol. 1, p. 17.

62. James S. Fishkin, *Justice, Equal Opportunity, and the Family* (New Haven: Yale University Press, 1983).

Chapter 3
How "Public Opinion" Became the Voice of the People

1. Shlomo Slonim, "The Electoral College at Philadelphia: The Evolution of an Ad Hoc Congress for the Selection of the President," *Journal of American History* 73 (June 1986): 35–59; quotation is from p. 57.

2. Henry Jones Ford, *The Rise and Growth of American Politics* (New York: Macmillan, 1898), pp. 213–214.

3. In terms of the values identified earlier, political equality and participation together are furthered by gains in popular control.

4. Neal R. Peirce and Lawrence D. Longley, *The People's President: The Electoral College in American History and the Direct Vote Alternative*. Rev. ed. (New Haven: Yale University Press, 1981), p. 49.

5. In spite of this image of deliberation at work, it is worth pointing out that the first party conventions nominated candidates by acclamation. The first national party

convention to have a real nomination struggle was the 1844 Democratic Convention, which unexpectedly nominated James K. Polk. I would like to thank Dean Burnham for this point.

6. Cited in William H. Riker, "The Senate and American Federalism" *American Political Science Review* 49 (June 1995): 452–469. This section has benefited greatly from Riker's insightful article.

7. Congressional Record, vol. 47, p. 1743 (June 7, 1911), cited in Riker, "Senate and American Federalism," p. 467.

8. William Bennett Munro, "'Such was the Man'—the Bryce that I Knew," in Robert Brooks, ed., *Bryce's* American Commonwealth: *Fiftieth Anniversary* (New York: Macmillan, 1939), pp. 204–235. The quotations are from p. 206.

9. James Bryce, *The American Commonwealth,* vol. 2 (New York: Macmillan, 1933), pp. 267, 268. Further references will be to this edition and will be cited parenthetically in the text.

10. For an excellent assessment, particularly of the influence of elites via the media, see John R. Zaller, *The Nature and Origins of Mass Opinion* (Cambridge: Cambridge University Press, 1992).

11. George Gallup, *The Pulse of Democracy: The Public Opinion Poll and How It Works* (1940; New York: Greenwood, 1968), p. 18; George Gallup, "Public Opinion in a Democracy." The Stafford Little Lectures. (Princeton: Princeton University Extension Fund, 1939), p. 6.

12. Gallup, "Public Opinion," pp. 6–7. "The successful candidate is frequently tempted to regard his election as a blanket endorsement of his entire program, although in point of fact, this may not express the real intentions of his supporters": Gallup, *Pulse of Democracy*, p. 18.

13. Gallup began with quota sampling and did not move to random sampling until after the debacle of the 1948 election, where he predicted Dewey over Truman.

14. Gallup, "Public Opinion," 14–15.

15. Ibid., p. 15.

16. Ibid.

17. John Brehm, *The Phantom Respondents: Opinion Surveys and Political Representation* (Ann Arbor: University of Michigan Press, 1993), p. 3.

18. Eugene Hartley, *Problems in Prejudice* (New York: Columbia University Press, 1946), pp. 10–12.

19. See George F. Bishop, Robert W. Oldendick, Alfred J. Tuchfarber and Stephen E. Bennett, "Pseudo-Opinions on Public Affairs," *Public Opinion Quarterly* 44 (1980): 198–208.

20. Philip E. Converse, "The Nature of Belief Systems in Mass Publics," in David E. Apter, ed., *Ideology and Discontent* (New York: Free Press, 1964), p. 245.

21. Philip E. Converse, "Attitudes and Non-Attitudes: Continuation of a Dialogue," in Edward R. Tufte, ed., *The Quantitative Analysis of Social Problems* (Reading, Mass.: Addison-Wesley, 1970), p. 171.

22. Ibid., p. 176.

23. W. Russell Neuman, *The Paradox of Mass Politics: Knowledge and Opinion and the American Electorate* (Cambridge, Mass.: Harvard University Press, 1986), p. 23.

24. See Michael W. Traugott, "The Impact of Media Polls on the Public," in Thomas E. Mann and Gary R. Orren, ed., *Media Polls in American Politics* (Washington, D.C.: Brookings Institution, 1992), pp. 125–149.

25. See Shanto Iyengar and Donald Kinder, *News that Matters: Television and American Opinion* (Chicago: University of Chicago Press, 1987).

26. See "Nine Days in America," *Economist* (London), May 8, 1976, p. 11.

27. Richard Morin, "What Informed Public Opinion? A Survey Trick Points Out the Hazards Facing Those Who Take the Nation's Pulse," *Washington Post National Weekly Edition,* April 10–16, 1995.

28. See Benjamin I. Page and Robert Y. Shapiro, *The Rational Public: Fifty Years of Trends in Americans' Policy Preferences* (Chicago: University of Chicago Press, 1992), pp. 17–23.

29. "Higher Learning in the Nation's Service." Carnegie Foundation for the Advancement of Teaching (Washington, D.C., 1981).

30. The phrase comes from James Russell Lowell in 1888 and is taken by Michael Kammen for the title of his book *A Machine That Would Go of Itself* (New York: Random House, 1986). Lowell is cited on p. 18.

31. See Thomas Grey, "Do We Have a Written Constitution?" *Stanford Law Review* 27 (1975): 703–718.

32. Principles can be distinguished from rules in terms of the kind of interpretation they require. For an illuminating discussion, see Ronald Dworkin, *Law's Empire* (Cambridge, Mass: Harvard University Press, 1986), chap. 1.

33. The phrase "derived from public opinion" comes from Samuel Williams, *The Natural and Civil History of Vermont* (Walpole, N.H.: Isaiah Thomas and David Carlisle, 1794), quoted in Gordon Wood, *The Creation of the American Republic, 1776–1787* (New York: Norton, 1969), p. 612.

34. Quoted in Wood, *Creation of the American Republic,* p. 533.

35. Max Farrand, ed., *The Records of the Federal Convention of 1787.* Rev. ed. 4 vols. (New Haven: Yale University Press, 1966), vol. 2, p. 476.

36. Wood, *Creation of the American Republic,* p. 342.

37. A Pennsylvania legislator, cited by William Nelson, *The Fourteenth Amendment: From Political Principle to Judicial Doctrine* (Cambridge, Mass: Harvard University Press, 1988), p. 94.

38. Bruce A. Ackerman, "The Storrs Lectures: Discovering the Constitution," *Yale Law Journal* 93 (1984): 1013–1072; see p. 1065.

39. See Bruce A. Ackerman, *We the People: Foundations* (Cambridge, Mass: Harvard University Press, 1991).

Chapter 4
Who Are the People?

1. Chilton Williamson, *American Suffrage: From Property to Democracy 1760–1860* (Princeton: Princeton University Press, 1960).

2. Quoted in Williamson, *American Suffrage*, p. 11.

3. Anthony Trollope, *Phineas Finn*, vol. 1 (London: Oxford University Press, 1949), p. 297.

4. Ibid., p. 312.

5. Quoted in Williamson, *American Suffrage*, p. 147.

6. Williamson, ibid., p. 117.

7. See Edmund Morgan, *American Slavery, American Freedom* (New York: Norton, 1975), p. 4.

8. Merrill D. Peterson, ed., *The Portable Thomas Jefferson* (New York: Penguin Books, 1975), p. 238.

9. Quoted in Willard Sterne Randall, *Thomas Jefferson: A Life* (New York: H. Holt, 1993), p. 277.

10. Peterson, *Portable Thomas Jefferson*, p. 188.

11. See Noble E. Cunningham, Jr., *The Life of Thomas Jefferson: In Pursuit of Reason* (New York: Ballantine, 1987), pp. 12–13.

12. Peterson, *Portable Thomas Jefferson*, p. 215.

13. Philip S. Foner, ed., *The Life and Writings of Frederick Douglass*, vol. 5 (New York: International Publishers, 1975), p. 401. My discussion of Frederick Douglass has been greatly enriched by Shelley Fisher Fishkin and Carla L. Peterson, "We Hold These Truths to be Self-Evident: The Rhetoric of Frederick Douglass's Journalism," in Eric J. Sundquist, ed., *Frederick Douglass: New Literary and Historical Essays* (Cambridge: Cambridge University Press, 1990), pp. 189–204.

14. Foner, *Life and Writings of Douglass*, pp. 401–403.

15. Ibid., pp. 403, 405. Douglass singles out one such July 4 speech, in particular, by a Mr. Choate.

16. "What to the Slave Is the Fourth of July?" Appendix in Frederick Douglass, *My Bondage and My Freedom* (New York: Arno, 1968), pp. 441–445; quotation is from pp. 443–444.

17. Ibid., p. 444.

18. Foner, *Life and Writings of Douglass*, p. 407.

19. Paul M. Angle, introduction, in Angle, ed., *The Complete Lincoln-Douglas Debates of 1858*. (Chicago: University of Chicago Press, 1991), pp. xxxviii–xxxix. All further references to the debates will be to this edition and will be cited parenthetically in the text.

20. Foner, *Life and Writings of Douglass*, pp. 407, 409.

21. Quoted in Garry Wills, *Inventing America: Jefferson's Declaration of Independence* (Garden City, N.Y.: Doubleday, 1978), p. xvi.

22. Also quoted by Douglass in Foner, *Life and Writings of Douglass,* pp. 409–410.

23. Harry V. Jaffa, *Crisis of the House Divided: An Interpretation of the Issues of the Lincoln-Douglas Debates* (1959; Seattle: University of Washington Press, 1973), p. 42.

24. Ibid., p. 25.

25. The Buchanan Democrats also received 5,071 votes, denying the Lincoln Republicans a majority. See Angle, *Lincoln-Douglas Debates,* p. xliv.

26. Michael W. McConnell, "The Forgotten Constitutional Moment," *Constitutional Commentary* 11 (Winter 1994): 115–144; quotation is from p. 129.

27. Booker T. Washington, quoted in W. E. B. du Bois, *The Souls of Black Folk,* in his *Writings:* The Suppression of the African Slave-Trade; The Souls of Black Folk; Dusk of Dawn; *Essays and Articles from* The Crisis, ed. Nathan Huggins (New York: Library of America, 1986), p. 393.

28. W. E. B. Du Bois, *Souls of Black Folk,* in ibid., 393.

29. Ibid., 404, 398–399.

30. Ibid., pp. 424, 425, 360, 364–365.

31. Ibid., p. 438.

32. Ibid., p. 404.

33. Alexis de Tocqueville, *Democracy in America,* ed. J. P. Mayer, trans. George Lawrence (Garden City, N.Y.: Anchor Doubleday, 1969), pp. 252–253n.

34. Charles W. Chesnutt, *Disfranchisement,* in Ulysses Lee, ed., *The Negro Problem: A Series of Articles by American Negroes of To-Day* (1903; New York: Arno, 1969), p. 84. Further references are to this edition and are cited parenthetically in the text.

35. Abigail M. Thernstrom, *Whose Votes Count? Affirmative Action and Minority Voting Rights* (Cambridge, Mass: Harvard University Press, 1987), p. 2.

36. See Chesnutt, *Disfranchisement,* p. 117.

37. Thernstrom, *Whose Votes?* p. 2.

38. Gerald N. Rosenberg, *The Hollow Hope: Can Courts Bring About Social Change?* (Chicago: University of Chicago Press, 1991), pp. 60–61.

39. Mark E. Rush, *Does Redistricting Make a Difference? Partisan Representation and Electoral Behavior* (Baltimore: Johns Hopkins University Press, 1993), p. 2. More generally on issues of racial redistricting, see the excellent paper by Mark E. Rush, "*Shaw v. Reno* and the Curious Evolution of Voting Rights Jurisprudence," presented at the Southwestern Political Science Association, San Antonio, Texas, March 1994.

40. Frank R. Parker, "Racial Gerrymandering and Legislative Reapportionment," in Chandler Davidson, ed., *Minority Vote Dilution* (Washington, D.C.: Howard University Press, 1984), pp. 85–117.

41. Parker, "Racial Gerrymandering," pp. 85–117; see esp. p. 87.

42. Ibid., p. 89.

43. 247 F. Supp. 96 (M.S. Ala. 1965); discussed in Parker, ibid., pp. 92–96.

44. Parker, ibid., pp. 96–99.

45. See Armand Derfner, "Vote Dilution and the Voting Rights Act Amendments of 1982," in Davidson, *Minority Vote Dilution,* pp. 145–166.

46. Thernstrom, *Whose Votes?* p. 3.

47. Chandler Davidson, "Minority Vote Dilution: An Overview," in Davidson, *Minority Vote Dilution,* pp. 8–9.

48. *Shaw v. Reno,* 113 S. Ct. 2816, 2826–2827 (1993).

49. See Daniel Polsby and Robert Popper, "Ugly: An Inquiry into the Problem of Racial Gerrymandering under the Voting Rights Act," *Michigan Law Review* 92 (December 1993), p. 652.

50. See Ronald Rogowski, "Representation in Political Theory and Law," *Ethics* 91 (April 1981): 395–430.

51. Quoted in June Sochen, *Herstory: A Record of the American Woman's Past* (Palo Alto, Calif.: Mayfield, 1982), p. 62.

52. Margaret Forster, *Significant Sisters: The Grassroots of Active Feminism* (New York: Oxford University Press, 1984), pp. 213–215.

53. Elizabeth Cady Stanton, "Speech to the Anniversary of the Anti-Slavery Society" (1860), in Ellen Carol DuBois, ed., *The Elizabeth Cady Stanton-Susan B. Anthony Reader* (Boston: Northeastern University Press, 1992), p. 81.

54. Stanton, *History of Woman's Suffrage,* vol. 1, p. 419, cited in DuBois, *Reader,* p. 11.

55. Forster, *Significant Sisters,* p. 209.

56. "The Declaration of Sentiments," in *The Concise History of Woman Suffrage,* ed. Paul Buhle and Mary Jo Buhle (Urbana: University of Illinois Press, 1979), p. 96.

57. Stanton, "Address Delivered at Seneca Falls," July 19, 1848, cited in DuBois, *Reader,* p. 32.

58. "Declaration of Sentiments," 94–95.

59. Ibid., p. 96.

60. Stanton, "Address of Welcome to the International Council of Women" March 25, 1888, cited in DuBois, *Reader,* p. 215.

61. Susan B. Anthony, cited in DuBois, *Reader,* p. 154.

62. Mike Cassidy, "Statue? Statue? Oh, You Mean that Fool Statue," *San Jose Mercury News,* January 30, 1994, p. 1B. I am grateful to Denny Crimmins for suggesting this example.

63. Quoted in Joe Rodriquez, "Serpent Wars," *San Jose Mercury News,* September 19, 1993, p. 7C.

64. Cassidy, "Statue? Statue?"

65. Anna Julia Cooper, *A Voice from the South* (New York: Oxford University Press, 1988), p. 163.

66. Ibid., pp. 163–164.

67. Ibid., p. 165.

68. See, for example, two classic studies: Samuel A. Stouffer, *Communism, Con-*

formity and Civil Liberties (New York: Doubleday, 1955), and James Prothro and C. W. Grigg, "Fundamental Principles of Democracy," *Journal of Politics* 22 (1960): 276–294.

69. See Michael Kammen, *A Machine That Would Go of Itself* (New York: Random House, 1986), where this is a central theme.

70. David Cannadine, "The British Monarchy, c. 1820–1977," in Eric Hobsbaum and Terence Ranger, eds., *The Invention of Tradition* (Cambridge: Cambridge University Press, 1983), pp. 142–143.

71. Ibid., p. 142.

72. See the classic discussion in Arthur M. Schlesinger, Jr., *The Imperial Presidency* (Boston: Houghton Mifflin, 1973), which focuses on foreign policy but also has more general implications

73. 310 U.S. 586, 596 (1940); 310 U.S. 586, 599 (1940); 310 U.S. 586, 600 (1940).

74. Justice Jackson, "Board of Education v. Barnette," reprinted in Robert Paul Wolff, ed., *Political Man and Social Man* (New York: Random House, 1966), p. 182.

75. Ibid., p. 189.

76. Ibid., p. 188.

Chapter 5

Giving the People Voice

1. Quoted in Harry A. Overstreet and Bonaro W. Overstreet, *Town Meeting Comes to Town* (New York: Harper and Row, 1938), p. 19.

2. Ibid., p. 25.

3. Overstreet and Overstreet, *Town Meeting*, p. 15.

4. Overstreet and Overstreet, ibid., p. 113.

5. Quoted in Neal R. Peirce, "Electronic Town Halls? Right On, Ro00," *National Journal,* June 6, 1992, p. 1367.

6. See James S. Fishkin, "Beyond Teledemocracy: America on the Line," *Responsive Community* 2: 3 (1992): 13–19.

7. *All Things Considered*, National Public Radio, November 2, 1992, transcript.

8. See Elizabeth Kolbert, "Perot to Hold His Own Vote, but This Time on Television," *New York Times,* March 20, 1993.

9. Michael Kelly, "The 1992 Campaign: Third-Party Candidate; Perot's Vision: Consensus by Computer," *New York Times,* June 6, 1992, sect. 1, p. 1.

10. Alexis de Tocqueville, *Democracy in America,* ed. J. P. Mayer, trans. George Lawrence (Garden City, N.Y.: Anchor Doubleday, 1969), p. 513. Further references are to this edition and are cited parenthetically in the text.

11. Robert D. Putnam, "The Prosperous Community: Social Capital and Public Affairs," *American Prospect* 13 (Spring 1993), p. 36.

12. Referendum voting is not required by law in Italy, and preference voting, where one indicates both party preference and the choice of a particular candidate, is

taken as an indicator of patron-client relations. See Robert D. Putnam, *Making Democracy Work: Civic Traditions in Modern Italy* (Princeton: Princeton University Press, 1993), pp. 91–97; quote on p. 98.

13. Putnam, "Prosperous Community," 35–36.

14. The classic discussion is Mancur Olson, *The Logic of Collective Action* (New York: Schocken, 1968).

15. Quoted in David R. Boldt, "The Civic Virtue of Singing Together," *Baltimore Sun*, September 7, 1994, p. 15A.

16. See James S. Coleman, Thomas Hoffer, and Sally Kilgore, *High School Achievement: Public, Catholic, and Private Schools Compared* (New York: Basic, 1982). See also the discussion of Ernie Cortes, below.

17. The quotations in this section from Ernie Cortes, Jr., are from his talk "Reweaving the Fabric: The Iron Rule and the IAF Strategy for Power and Politics," in Henry G. Cisneros, ed., *Interwoven Destinies: Cities and the Nation* (New York: Norton, 1993); I have also relied on his "Politics of Social Capital," *Texas Observer,* January 29, 1993, pp. 16–17, and personal discussions.

18. Coleman, Hoffer, and Kilgore, *High School Achievement.*

19. See James P. Comer, *School Power: Implications of an Intervention Project* (New York: Free Press, 1980).

20. Putnam, *Making Democracy Work*, p. 167.

21. Ibid., p. 168.

22. David Wessel, "Two Unusual Lenders Show How 'Bad Risks' Can Be Good Business," *Wall Street Journal,* June 23, 1992.

23. David W. Moore, *The Superpollsters: How to Measure and Manipulate Public Opinion in America* (New York: Four Walls Eight Windows, 1992), p. 45.

24. Michael Schudson, *Discovering the News: A Social History of American Newspapers* (New York: Basic, 1978).

25. David Broder, "Democracy and the Press," *Washington Post,* January 3, 1990, p. A 15.

26. Jay Rosen, "Politics, Vision, and the Press: Toward a Public Agenda for Journalism," in *The New News and the Old News: The Press and Politics in the 1990s* (New York: Twentieth Century Fund, 1990), pp. 7–8.

27. Ibid., p. 12.

28. Ibid.

29. Ibid., p. 13.

30. Ibid., p. 14.

31. Edward D. Miller, "The Charlotte Project: Helping Citizens Take Back Democracy," *The Poynter Papers,* no. 4 (St. Petersburg, Fla.: Poynter Institute, 1994), p. 45.

32. Ibid., p. 87.

33. Ibid., p. 21.

34. Neal R. Peirce, "Charlotte Launches Unconventional Crime Crusade," *Times-Picayune* (New Orleans), July 5, 1994, p. B 7.

35. The Kennedy-Romney debate of October 25, 1994, received a rating of 42.3 percent of the television households, as compared to 38.7 percent for the 1994 Super Bowl or 41.7 percent for the O. J. Simpson car chase. See Frederic M. Biddle, "Senate Race Debate Proves a Winner in TV Ratings," *Boston Globe,* October 27, 1994.

36. Richard Morin, "Newspapers Ask Their Readers What's Important," *Charlotte Observer* (North Carolina), June 14, 1994.

37. Jeff Kampelman and I developed the initial proposal, based on my article "The Case for a National Caucus: Taking Democracy Seriously," *Atlantic Monthly,* August 1988, pp. 16–18.

38. Rosen, "Politics, Vision, and the Press," p. 26.

39. David Mathews, *Politics for People: Finding a Responsible Public Voice* (Urbana: University of Illinois Press, 1994), p. 108.

40. Ibid., p. 108.

41. Ibid., p. 109.

42. For a more detailed account, see my "Britain Experiments with the Deliberative Poll," *Public Perspective* 5:5 (1994): 27–29, and the accompanying article by Norman Webb, "What, Really, Should We Think about 'The Deliberative Poll?'" in the same issue.

43. See the discussion in chapter 3: "Is there a Rational Public?" above.

Afterword

The National Issues Convention and Beyond

1. Since the National Issues Convention, I have filed an application to register Deliberative Polling™ as a trademark. The University of Texas has established a Center for Deliberative Polling™ which will support research and applications of the process.

2. There are some key people whom I would like to thank for making the NIC possible. Charly Walker served as senior adviser to the project and co-chair of the NIC Advisory Board. Charly's efforts made the event possible and made it far more substantive when it did happen. Without his help this would still be a thought experiment. Jim Lehrer, Dan Werner, and Les Crystal of MacNeil/Lehrer Productions showed extraordinary judgment and leadership in bringing an idea to reality on television. Norman Bradburn of the National Opinion Research Center had the wisdom to see the NIC's value as a social science experiment and provided invaluable help throughout. Phil Converse and the entire technical review committee guided us through one difficult issue after another. Bob Luskin has been a skilled and insightful collaborator throughout. Bob Kingston of the Kettering Foundation did more than anyone else to make the Deliberative Poll an event that truly contributed to public deliberation. Noelle McAfee, assistant director of the NIC, imaginatively combined substantive insight and organizational ability. President Robert Berdahl and Vice President Ed Sharpe of the University of Texas had the vision to commit the University to a most unusual project— part social science experiment, part public event. Not many university administrators

would have taken the step that they did. Last, I want to thank my family, particularly my wife, Shelley Fisher Fishkin, and my father-in-law, Milton Fisher, who provided me with crucial support.

3. At this writing, my collaborators and I have completed eight Deliberative Polls. For summary data on all eight experiments see Appendix C.

4. I am working with Robert Luskin of the University of Texas, Norman Bradburn and Ken Rosinski of the NORC at the University of Chicago; and Roger Jowell, Becky Gray, and Alison Park of Social and Community Planning Research (SCPR) in London. We are planning a series of separate scholarly articles in which the data will be analyzed systematically. I am grateful to these collaborators for their help on all the research reported here. In addition, I would like to thank Chris Bratcher and Han Dorussen for very skilled research assistance here at the University of Texas.

5. Participation in the NIC small group discussions required at least some familiarity with English. In the later Texas utility polls we experimented successfully with bilingual moderators who provided translation.

6. These interviews were conducted in person in November and December 1995 and early January 1996.

7. I would like to thank Sally Murphy and Woody Carter of NORC for their resourcefulness in dealing with the unprecedented challenges of getting a national random sample of respondents to Austin.

8. Steven A. Holmes, "Chronicling the Shaping of Opinions," *New York Times,* December 3, 1995.

9. The sixty-six items include fifty-six that consider policy alternatives explicitly and ten that are classified as empirical premises of public policy, such as "Free trade helps all countries through increased trade and faster growth in living standards."

10. On fifty-eight of the sixty-six policy items (88 percent) there were no statistically significant differences at the .01 level.

11. For example, on the question of whether it is very useful, somewhat useful, or not useful at all to limit sex and violence on television, both participants and nonparticipants had a clear majority for "very useful," and both ranked the three options the same, but among nonrespondents, the majority was 61 percent, while among respondents, the majority was 54 percent. The difference between participants and nonparticipants is significant at the .05 level, but it does not reflect any real difference in their substantive views.

12. Public Agenda, the National Issues Forums, and the Kettering Foundation all made great contributions to the success of the NIC. Keith Melville at Public Agenda and Bob Kingston at Kettering both brought invaluable insight and experience to the problem of adapting discussion materials to the needs of the NIC.

13. Barbara Jordan was a great help to the convention and it was a terrible blow to all of us when she died on the eve of the NIC.

14. I want to thank Karl Rove for his advice and extraordinary assistance in dealing with the Republican presidential candidates. The convention would not have been

a success without his help. I also want to especially thank Bill Galston for his help and advice on the Democratic side.

15. Senator Lugar and Vice President Gore came, along with six experts—on the economy, Lester Thurow of MIT and William Niskanen, head of the Cato Institute; on family issues, Kenda Bartelett of Concerned Women for America and Tom Andrews, president of People for the American Way; and on foreign affairs, Donald McHenry, U.S. Ambassador to the U.N. during the Carter administration, and Charles Lichenstein, former Reagan administration official. Presidential candidates Phil Gramm, Steve Forbes, and Lamar Alexander participated in the dialogue by answering questions from the sample via satellite. The three-hour Republican broadcast on Saturday night was repeated on the following Sunday afternoon, and the one-hour dialogue with Vice President Gore was broadcast live Sunday morning and by tape Sunday evening. A ninety-minute wrap-up documentary with the results of the Deliberative Poll and a taped account of the small group discussions was broadcast the following Friday evening, January 26, 1996. Hence the convention received a total broadcast time of nine and one half hours, counting the repeated broadcasts.

16. Twenty-six of the sixty-six items (39 percent) changed significantly at the .01 level.

17. Five of these six items changed significantly at the .05 level and four changed significantly at the .01 level.

18. These sixty-six items do not include the six civic engagement items on which there was even more change. At least 50 percent of respondents offered different answers on four out of six (67 percent) of these items and at least 40 percent of respondents changed positions on five out of six (83 percent).

19. John T. Campbell and Julian C. Stanley, *Experimental and Quasi-Experimental Designs for Research* (Chicago: Rand McNally, 1963).

20. The Deliberative Poll in the 1997 British general election also includes questions coordinated with telephone polls of separate samples.

21. I would like to thank Roger Jowell for providing Appendix D.

22. This extraordinary commitment of airtime reflected the vision of Ervin Duggan, the president of PBS, and of Jim Lehrer, who served as anchor for the entire event.

23. The American Press Institute convened a seminar led by Jay Rosen that met before and after the convention. This seminar assessed the NIC's potential for contributing to public journalism. The Poynter Institute for Media Studies held a symposium on the eve of the convention in the LBJ Library to air conflicting views about what it might all mean.

24. This search included variants such as Deliberative Poll and Deliberative Polling as well as of my name.

25. For example, WHD-YFM and the *Philadelphia Inquirer* hosted "CITIZEN VOICES '96," billed as "A Local Version of the National Issues Convention" in February 1996. In September 1996, another Philadelphia group held what it called "A National Issues Convention for Youth" modeled on the NIC.

26. Max McCombs of the University of Texas department of journalism is editing a volume of essays on this topic.

27. See Kenneth A. Rasinski, "A Field Experiment to Evaluate Viewing the National Issues Convention on Television, Part I: Effects on Trust in Government," a paper presented at the Annual Meeting of the American Association for Public Opinion Research, Salt Lake City, May 16–19, 1996.

28. Tom Brazaitas, "Ordinary People Learn They Are the Experts," *Plain Dealer* (Cleveland), January 28, 1996.

29. Michael Tackett, "Table Talk Reveals Worry on Economy: Citizens Air Common Concerns in Texas," *Chicago Tribune,* January 21, 1996.

30. Debra Goldman, "Focus Group USA: The Austin Athenians Show the 1996 Election Is Not Only a Contest Between Candidates, but a Fight Over the Dialogue of Politics Itself," *Adweek,* February 12, 1996, pp. 10–13.

31. For criticism of the NIC in terms of the Hawthorne effect, see for example Everett Carl Ladd, "The NIC Poll Revisited: Magic Town and Jimmy Stewart Demonstrate the Hawthorne Effect," *Public Perspective* 7, no. 3 (April–May 1996): 16.

32. The symposium was held October 16, 1996, at Channel 4 in London, and the panelists included Worcester, journalist Peter Kellner, Roger Jowell of SCPR, television presenter Sheena MacDonald, and myself.

33. Richard Morin, "Using the Brits as a Test Case," *Washington Post National Weekly Edition,* May 12, 1997.

34. Fiona Cairns, Barbara McMahon, "Lib-Dems Set for 45 Seats in Best Result for 70 Years," *Evening Standard,* May 2, 1997.

35. Robert Lea, "Gain and Pain in the Great L10M Gamble," *Evening Standard,* May 2, 1997.

36. "UK Govt Did Not Campaign Enough on Economy—Clarke," Reuters, May 1, 1997.

37. Youssef M. Ibrahim, "Britain '97: Rich, Poor and a Little in Between," *New York Times,* April 29, 1997.

38. As noted on page 82, Converse's initial discovery of nonattitudes came, in part, with analyses of a question involving the government's role in electric power.

39. I would like to thank Dennis Thomas, former head of the PUC of Texas, for the insight that Deliberative Polling would find a suitable application in integrated resource planning. With his help, and that of an enlightened management at Central and South West, and the able assistance of Will Guild at Delta Strategies, we were able to make the utility polls a success.

40. See, for example, the press release of the Environmental Defense Fund congratulating the utilities for following the judgments of the people in the Deliberative Polling process. Press release, February 2, 1997.

41. There were certain differences in the briefings having to do with the varying circumstances in the three service territories. For example, there were differences in the cost of buying and transporting power and in proximity to Mexico, which played a role in the discussions.

INDEX